THE ART OF PREVENTING STUPID

THE ART OF PREVENTING STUPID

HOW TO BUILD A STRONGER BUSINESS STRATEGY THROUGH BETTER RISK MANAGEMENT

MATTHEW NEILL DAVIS, Esq.

AN INC.
ORIGINAL

This publication is designed to provide accurate and authoritative information in regard to the subject matter covered. It is sold with the understanding that the publisher and author are not engaged in rendering legal, accounting, or other professional services. If legal advice or other expert assistance is required, the services of a competent professional should be sought.

An Inc. Original
New York, New York
www.anincoriginal.com

Distributed by Greenleaf Book Group

For ordering information or special discounts for bulk purchases, please contact Greenleaf Book Group at PO Box 91869, Austin, TX 78709, 512.891.6100.

Design and composition by Greenleaf Book Group and Kim Lance
Cover design by Greenleaf Book Group and Kim Lance
Image Copyright Arbuz, 2018. Used under license from Shutterstock.com

Publisher's Cataloging-in-Publication data is available.

Print ISBN: 978-1-7325102-1-0

eBook ISBN: 978-1-7325102-2-7

Part of the Tree Neutral® program, which offsets the number of trees consumed in the production and printing of this book by taking proactive steps, such as planting trees in direct proportion to the number of trees used: www.treeneutral.com

Printed in the United States of America on acid-free paper

19 20 21 22 23 24 25   10 9 8 7 6 5 4 3 2 1

First Edition

I dedicate this book to my brilliant and beautiful wife, Allison.
She is a partner who makes everything in my life better.

Contents

Table of Figures

Acknowledgments

First, to my wonderful wife, Allison: Remember it is a partnership. Oh, and to all those pesky kids of ours, who put up with my writing: Emma, Meg, Henry, Luke, and Sally.

To Maggie Lichtenberg and Cynde Christie for helping craft this book.

To Professor-now-Congressman David Loebsack for teaching me that I can write.

To Professor Ted Lowi for teaching me to think categorically.

And to my mentors: Rjon Robins, Kristen David, Henry Harlow, Chris Anderson, Chris Dyson, and Terrence Fogarty, thank you for reminding me of my potential.

To our "Home Team": Jaime Walker, Nicole Winfield, Ashley Morey, Zach Keen, Kaleb Boese, Katie Myers, Katie Thomas, Bonnie Espinoza, Sara Hill, Jane Ann Dixon, Ivey Dyson, and Joe Titterington.

To Kevin Friesen, Molly Helm, Christina Mathews, Catherine Freshley, Randy Greene, and Dave Schlitter for all the support and great advice.

To my beta readers: Joseph Chiummiento, Rob Cummins, Jeff Gwin, Greg Hodgen, Bert Mackie, Bond Payne, Weber Player, John Walker, Aaron Harmon, and Mike Wright.

And finally, to Groendyke Transport, especially John Groendyke, Greg Hodgen, Steve Feldhaus, and the rest of the senior management team for showing us how a fantastic company runs and how it can change thousands of lives.

Learning the Art

WE ALL KNOW THE AWFUL FEELING A STUPID MISTAKE BRINGS as your palm slaps your forehead and you agonize over the reality that you never should have let this happen. The reason for this sinking feeling is that deep down we know our problems are generally either preventable or can be better managed if we are simply prepared. This book is about building a better mousetrap for dealing with the risks that can arise in your business. It is about empowering you to be better able to focus on your strengths and opportunities because you *have* managed the threats and weaknesses inherent in all business.

We often let managing our lives and running our businesses get in the way of making the time to take those necessary steps to ward off possible problems. Inconvenience, procrastination, laziness, or just not knowing where to start—these can all lead to putting off the examination of your business's threats and weaknesses. What this book offers is an incisive and efficient method that we call Preventing Stupid, designed to help you avoid not only the horrible feeling that stupid mistakes elicit but also the very serious impacts they have on your bottom line and peace of mind. By using this method, you will build resistance to mistakes directly into your business, just as your body must ward off or react to disease. That is why we call the result your Business Immune System™ (BIS).

The key is to build a system that enables you effectively to manage your risk efficiently. The prominent twentieth-century management consultant W. Edwards Deming once noted, "A bad system will beat a good person every time."[1] What he emphasized is that having a system in place to get the work done right is critical. If there is no system, then there is the strong possibility that even if the work gets done, it will be haphazard and subject to the vicissitudes of human failings. Of course, systems have their problems too, but they are better than the alternative. This holds true for a business trying to manage its potential problems as well.

All problems start as potentialities, some of which develop into distractions of varying degrees that prevent you from achieving your business goals. Once you understand how the Preventing Stupid process works and understand the attributes of the individual problems, you will be a step ahead in preventing and managing them. Then, when you grasp both the systemic origins of problems and the systems particular to every business, your acumen and ability will increase considerably; as a result, your business will be much safer and hopefully more successful.

Even with this knowledge in hand, business owners still face a myriad of potential and present problems that can obscure their vision and distract them from building their businesses. In fact, merely dealing with the daily issues of the business can impede progress and profitability when problems go unchecked. Meanwhile the worry and apprehension regarding potential problems can eat away at the business owner's ability to concentrate. To combat this situation, in chapter 6, I introduce the Preventing Stupid Method to help business owners cut through the fog of uncertainty. The Preventing Stupid

Method utilizes the principle that three basic questions outline the three primary reasons that a business owner fails to protect his or her business from potential problems.

Next, I show you how three simple questions applied to your business's systems will open the door to effective and efficient prevention and management of problems. The result is a calmer, more confident business owner or manager who can turn his or her focus into creating leads for a more profitable business and who can seize opportunities rather than wallowing in problems that never should have made it to the surface.

Neatly categorizing and prioritizing present and potential threats and weaknesses is just the first step of your rigorous business analysis. The important questions detailing how to efficiently prevent or manage these potential and present problems remain unanswered. The Preventing Stupid Method focuses on these very questions, in addition to the identification and categorization of your potential problems, so that you can start to build your Business Immune System.

Building your BIS begins with the categorization of your potential problems, thereby enabling you to prioritize the threats to your business success based on both the likelihood of the development of those problems and their probable severity. From that vantage point, you can clearly see and effectively combat the three ways you might otherwise fail to protect your business. With time and practice, building and maintaining your BIS becomes second nature. However, as your business grows, you must continue to apply the Preventing Stupid Method to identify new threats coming your way.

Your understanding of the nature and origins of problems in general is critical to your business success, so I begin this book by outlining the subjective nature of problems. This information will also help you identify your goals so that you can start to anticipate any threats to them.

I own and run a legal and consulting firm that currently handles problem prevention and management for companies ranging from small family businesses to large regional ones. We call our services "customized legal departments" (CLD), because we integrate our services into our clients' businesses to build them legal departments suited to their needs. We then serve on their management team as their general counsel. We do this either in a comprehensive manner or on an à la carte basis for any of the eight areas of general-counsel responsibility for which they have a need. In effect, we wear two hats: we serve both as a senior manager and as the company's primary attorney. We work on preset time and expense budgets so that we can teach our clients to work within those financial constraints, while at the same time making problem prevention a core part of their businesses. This provides our clients with cost-effective, responsive, and highly competent legal counsel and a healthy BIS as well. It also allows us to sharpen our skill sets on a continual basis to meet the ongoing business needs of our clients by comparing notes across the board.

Big corporations typically have in-house general counsel to help management make proactive, smart decisions. These company attorneys are responsible for looking forward and advising the management on the prevention of stupid mistakes that can injure the company. While big companies have the luxury of being able to afford to keep such attorneys on staff, small companies rarely can afford this privilege. Small and medium-sized companies need good, forward-looking legal counsel every bit as much as the big companies do.

My firm helps fill the gap by providing the same advantages that the big companies have in a way that the smaller businesses can afford and that meets their needs. While the businesses I will use for illustration in this book are small, family-owned concerns, the principles of the Preventing Stupid Method hold true for businesses of all sizes.

After twenty years as a general practice attorney, I had an epiphany that kick-started my firm's commitment to CLD services: One of the firm's clients, a husband-and-wife team, were running a good-sized oil field contracting business. By superior organization and an insistence on quality workmanship, they landed the plum jobs with the best companies. They were making a substantial income; and my clients generally only contacted me, as their lawyer, when they had a problem. That is the key point to understand—they called me *when* problems occurred but not beforehand. That is, until one day when we were discussing a pressing problem and I stumbled on a major chink in the armor protecting their operations, livelihood, and future.

They had thirty or so loaded-down Ford F-550 trucks out on the rural highways and country roads every day. Almost in passing, I asked how much insurance they had and learned that their policy was only $2 million. That may or may not sound like a lot to you, but understanding the potential tort cases this type of business can become embroiled in, I was in shock. In fact, I was horrified, as I both admire and care deeply about these clients. They built the American dream from scratch. Their children will have opportunities far beyond what most parents ever dream about for their children. And all of this was in jeopardy, if even one of those drivers ever made an error and caused a catastrophic car wreck.

I stopped the ongoing conversation and immediately explained the reasons why the $2 million policy was not nearly enough for their needs. I then described the potential consequences of a claim against their company in excess of the $2 million limit. It was a sobering moment for them. Frankly, it was for me, as well. I had had numerous opportunities to prevent rather than to fix this vulnerability. This incident caught my attention and made me realize that if I wanted to make a real difference in my clients' lives, my firm needed to change its focus from being reactive to being proactive. These clients, incidentally some of my favorite people, had the proverbial knife at their throats, and none of us had caught it because we had not asked the right questions in a systematic way designed to catch vulnerabilities like this one.

Within a few days, they resolved the problem and the insurance limits shot up to a level sufficient to protect the company. It was not costly, nor was it time-consuming to fix. We had simply missed the need because we did not have a system in place to catch it. Of course, the accident did happen, in a split second, when one of their trucks hydroplaned and accidentally crossed the centerline on a two-lane highway. It was horrible. The parents of the two surviving children died in the new truck they had just purchased. The company's owner was in surgery when the accident occurred, so it was left to me, to the insurance agent, and to the owner's key man to handle the initial regrouping of the company at the time. We were able to settle the case without litigation. Fortunately, we had that insurance in place; the settlement required was for several times the prior policy limits.

I still get chills when I think about that chain of events. Every one of us continues to grieve the accident. Beyond that, my clients and I were grateful that we were able to provide financially for the survivors of the accident. It also instilled in me a driving need to prevent my clients from making mistakes that have the potential to cost them everything for which they have worked.

The mistake of underinsuring the company happened due to a failure of defense, because my clients were so busy playing offense. As their lawyer, I failed, and although I caught the vulnerability just in time, that was not good enough for me. Preventing the disaster to the company was not burdensome. It just required some forethought and a few minutes of slowing down to ask the right questions.

The problem facing most businesses is that, like my clients, owners are so preoccupied with moving forward, they never make the time to take these defensive measures. To remedy this pervasive situation, I set out on a mission to develop not only a practice but also a system to help business owners prevent these types of problems, so that they can be free to grow their businesses. This book details the system that I developed and that my firm employs to help our clients achieve the security they need.

When you set out to find the answer to a question, sometimes the answer falls right into your lap. I happened to be reading a book called *The Checklist Manifesto* by Atul Gawande.[2] He mentions, almost in passing, a study proving there are only two ways to fail: through ignorance or through ineptitude. I thought about his concept and decided that while almost correct, it overlooks catastrophes. If we know there are only three ways to fail, then why can't businesses take organized steps to prevent failure? I now had the initial building blocks to my system.

Then, I applied this idea to something I already knew: legal problems are the tip of the iceberg. They are a function of oversights in every business. The legal problems that brought clients to my office were actually symptoms of dysfunction in at least one of the seven systems common to all businesses. These include

- the owner;
- the personnel;
- the production;
- the physical plant;
- the metrics, including measurements of production and finance;
- the marketing; and
- the sales.

From that vantage point, I was able to recognize the similarities between businesses and organisms—that they all rely on properly functioning systems to be healthy and run correctly. Upon further reflection, I realized that we all have an immune system interwoven into the systems of our bodies that helps protect us from illness. So, I wondered how I could create a risk management and prevention tool that worked like a body's immune system.

The light bulb clicked on and right then, using an airline napkin as my notepad, I cross-referenced the three reasons to fail with the working parts of a business; and the basic idea of the Business Immune System Report (BISR) was born. By looking into their weaknesses, we can determine where businesses are prone to fail. I had it! I had an easy-to-understand method to help business owners change the way they think about identifying and preventing problems in their businesses.

This is the tool my firm now uses to analyze businesses. We use it as a report card and give an A–F grade corresponding to the strength of our clients' BISs, based on the extensive list of best business practices that my firm developed. It clearly and concisely categorizes the threats to a business. Then through the grade assigned, the report prioritizes the systems of the business that require preventive work, or current problems needing correction. The following is a report with examples of problems rather than grades:

BUSINESS IMMUNE SYSTEM REPORT: FAILURE EXAMPLES			
	CATASTROPHE	**IGNORANCE**	**INEPTITUDE**
Management	Owner Is Disabled in Car Wreck	Owner Does Not Know Key Skill Set	Owner Has Not Preserved Cash for Payday
Personnel	Key Person Dies	Team Does Not Have Required Skills	Owner Has Overlooked Key Job Function
Production	Computers or Registers Crash	Team Is Improperly Trained	Job Functions Are Repeatedly Performed Incorrectly
Plant	Fire Burns Down Plant	Company Has Purchased Wrong Size of Building	Rent Is Not Paid on Time
Metrics	Major Data Loss due to Computer Crash	Good Tax Strategy Not Developed	Company Has Failed to Maintain Measurements on Production
Marketing	Horrible Press due to Car Wreck by Driver	Key Customers Not Identified	Reaching Out to Wrong Customers
Sales	Key Meeting Is Missed by Salesperson	Salesperson Is Not Prepared to Answer Key Objections to a Deal	Failure to Call Customers Back

Figure 1: Business Immune System Report: Failure Examples

The problems mentioned in figure 1 are just a few examples of the issues that a business can face. The BISR is merely the first step in building the system for preventing such problems. When we work with a client to grade these twenty-one potential areas of threats to their business, the result is a report that shows them, in an easy-to-understand way, where we need to focus our efforts to protect their company. With this in hand, I realized how simple it was to protect a business. In fact, I decided it was so simple that, frankly, it was stupid not to do so, and I started using the term "preventing stupid" to apply to the first step of recognizing and categorizing the threats to a business's success. The second step is to apply time-proven management and legal strategies to build your BIS. Ultimately, I use the word "stupid" because it is highly motivational to people who are willing to improve, learn, and change. Nobody wants to be stupid, particularly high-functioning entrepreneurs set on changing the world and making a fortune. However, this cannot happen if you spend your time fixing problems rather than preventing them.

Most business owners are exceptionally skilled at what they do, whether it is blue-collar or white-collar work. You may be the star quarterback of the information-technology or plumbing world, but that does not mean you know how to manage risk. More commonly, business owners love plying their trade so much that they often neglect taking the steps to protect it. Previously, I showed how a failure to prepare for a catastrophe could have destroyed my client's company, or, at the very least, severely set back years of progress. That is just one example of how failing to ask the right questions about defense can ruin a business.

In this book, you will learn the Preventing Stupid Method as well as how to build your business's BIS. First, however, we are going to delve into a little abstract thought on the nature and origin of problems; after all, problems are the subject of this book, and you need to understand them if you are hoping to prevent them. We will then briefly examine the systems common to all businesses. Next, we will examine the area that business owners frequently fail to recognize. Then, we will turn our attention to why the Preventing Stupid Method works, and we will do this by providing an analytical framework for examining your business and then building your BIS to stop the stupid mistakes before they become problems (or, if they are unpreventable, make them manageable). Then, we will discuss when to begin the Preventing Stupid Method for startup companies. Finally, we follow up with a thorough examination of catastrophes, ignorance, and ineptitude—first generally, and then by fictional examples of ongoing businesses.

Let me be clear: you do not run a business on just preventing stupid, but you most likely will not have a business to run for the long term without doing it. This book is about changing your mind regarding how you should run your business. The first point I stress is that you do not have to be smart; just do not be stupid. Part of this book teaches you how to see your stupid mistakes before you make them, and then it prepares you to deal with them. This book will teach you how to process information to capitalize rapidly on opportunities, rather than miring in the muck of problems. If you can get to the point where you routinely avoid the dangers and take advantage of the opportunities, you are going to look smart, even if you really just prevented stupid.

In particular, this book is about changing how you think so you can run your business with confidence, effectiveness, and profitability. If you are a struggling entrepreneur, this book will help you weed out the stupid mistakes that you are already making so you can get on with making your fortune. If you are already running a successful business, changing how you think about it will make it easier, more profitable, and more secure. In either case, the goal is to change the way you think about your business—to align yourself with the Preventing Stupid Method of identifying the threats to your success so that you end up with a healthy BIS that protects your bottom line and peace of mind. Once you get this mindset and choose to prevent stupid, with a little luck, you should end up where you want to be, with financial security and personal freedom.

CHAPTER SUMMARY

- ✓ For a business to run smoothly, each system must function properly.

- ✓ The Business Immune System works as a risk-management tool to analyze twenty-one areas where businesses need work to prevent disaster.

- ✓ To prevent stupid, business owners must recognize and categorize threats to their business and, subsequently, build a Business Immune System to prevent these threats from becoming catastrophes.

- ✓ Problems are difficult to recognize, categorize, and analyze. However, problems are a function of goals. In other words, if a business owner possesses a goal, whether it is to grow the business or change internal operations, he or she will inevitably face obstacles to success. Thus, it is imperative that business owners have tools to handle and prevent problems.

The Four Key Attributes of Problems

IN THE 1964 CASE *JACOBELLIS V. OHIO*, UNITED STATES Supreme Court justice Potter Stewart described his test for obscenity by stating, "I know it when I see it." Unfortunately, most business owners would say the same about their problems—they know them when they see them. It is not that simple. Problems are a more complex subject, and understanding their nature, degree, and type opens the door to both preventing them and managing them when they are unavoidable. Additionally, considering which of the existing potential problems are more likely to happen builds yet another layer of robustness to your skill set in managing problems.

Problems do not exist in a vacuum. In fact, they cannot exist without the goals that define them. When you establish a goal, you also establish the set of potential problems that stands between you and your ability to reach your goal. Consequently, goals and problems are inextricable. You cannot have a problem without an objective. They are both subjective and dependent. Problems do not happen without a person wanting to do something. Even then, the degree of the problem depends on the goal of that person. Ultimately, the type of the problem is a function of that person's intent.

Imagine that I wanted to go for a drive, just to get out of town. I set my goal—to drive to a bigger city. I live in Enid, Oklahoma, where my family has lived since the Cherokee Strip Land Run in 1893. It is a comfortable place to live, and you can find 90 percent of what you need there, but sometimes you need to go to a bigger market. Enid is an hour and a half to two hours from Oklahoma City, Tulsa, or Wichita. I frequently visit or fly out of all three. I know my way around, and I do not have a preference between them for a simple day trip. My goal is to just go somewhere and enjoy the day.

I head east out of Enid on US 412 and initially choose Tulsa as my destination. When I get to the intersection with I-35, I discover that the Cimarron Turnpike heading east to Tulsa is closed. There is no acceptable alternate route to Tulsa. I now have another choice; I can turn south to Oklahoma City or north to Wichita. I do not have a problem at this point, however, because my goal has not been frustrated or impeded. My options are still intact, and I can achieve my goal by choosing which off-ramp to take.

If we take the same scenario and change my goal, then the entire nature of the road closure changes. Presume that my reason for going to Tulsa is that I have a family member dying in a hospital. In fact, his death is imminent. I want to get there to pay my final respects; therefore, it is important to me to get there quickly. When I come upon the road closure, it now presents a problem to me. There are no other direct routes to Tulsa, and the only alternative is going to add an hour to my trip.

The change in my goal altered the nature of the road closure. In the first scenario, it did not matter. It was not a problem. In the second example, however, it could mean the difference between my getting to the hospital in time or not. The very existence of a problem is a function of the will to accomplish something.

This brings us to the first attribute of a problem: it is completely subjective. A beach bum has no shirt, no shoes, and no problems. Of course, he still needs to figure out how to get food, clothing, and shelter. I know this is a bit of an exaggeration, but it makes a simple point: the lack of ambition defines the lack of problems. Conversely, if you have ambition, you are going to have problems. When my team and I work with our clients to resolve current or potential problems, we first ask specially designed questions to determine what their goals are. Once our client's goals are established, we can tell them what their potential problems are, based on those goals.

A business owner has a multitude of potential problems and, very likely, many existent problems. The sole reason is that the business owner is trying to accomplish something. Every one of us in business defines our goals and intentions; and again, by doing so, we also define our potential problems. This is exactly why foreseeing and managing the obstacles to business success is possible. Consequently, the task is reverse engineering the problems to learn how to prevent them in an efficient manner.

The goal does not have to be elaborate or grandiose. Many goals are as simple as just making it to the next day. For instance, presume you are forty-five and healthy, living a normal life with a normal job. You do not have any particular ambitions; you simply want to make it through the day and be happy. That statement just defined both the intention and the set of potential problems. Now, presume that you are suddenly out of food and money. While that, in and of itself, is not going to end your life in the course of a day, it likely will frustrate your will to be happy, because the hunger will be an irritation.

Many people live with the simple goal of just getting through life. There are also plenty of businesses run with the same intent—just getting by and providing a comfortable living for the owner, without any set goals for growing the business. It does not matter whether your goals are lofty or humble; they all set the stage for your problems. Thus, problems are wholly subjective. And because they are, we can identify them before they happen.

However, not all problems are equally disastrous, which brings us to the issue of prioritizing. I have a quick method of explaining this concept to my clients, and it involves using just two words to describe the distinction: "hassle" and "problem." They understand that a hassle is a nuisance. A hassle is resolvable within the normal course of business. It is an annoyance but not particularly difficult, expensive, or time-consuming to deal with. Problems, on the other hand, are a more serious matter; they are a real threat to the business owner's time, money, or reputation.

There is no quantitative science behind this distinction, but it is easily understandable. Once people have it explained to them, they realize that while they would rather not have any hassles, they are preferable to having problems. Regardless of where the issue falls on my problem-hassle continuum, there are many different names for problems:

- setback
- disaster
- failure
- issue
- trouble

- screw up
- catastrophe
- breakdown
- malfunction

All these words presuppose that something is not working correctly. However, these terms alone do not convey a clear sense of the severity of blockage. The common currency is that the goal has been frustrated. The word "disaster" can indicate something more severe than a "screw up," but the exact meaning of these two terms in relation to business problems remains dependent on a person's intent.

My team recognizes that there are varying degrees of importance to problems; hence, the more severe problems on the continuum are the ones that deserve the most attention. The goal is to develop clarity of thought about problems so that we prevent or manage them. Thus, in managing problems, it is very useful to formulate a subjective list of where the potential problem falls on a scale. For instance, a business might develop a range on a one-to-ten scale like this:

SAMPLE BUSINESS PROBLEM SEVERITY SCALE	
1	Hot Check
2	Small Unpaid Receivable
3	Small Lost Customer
4	Bad Press
5	Small-Claims Suit
6	Loss of Key Employee
7	Bankruptcy Reorganization
8	Major Lawsuit
9	Insolvency
10	Liquidation

Figure 2: Sample Business Problem Severity Scale

Making such distinctions is not particularly complicated, but it is critically useful. Business owners do it in their heads every day when they judge whether an issue is a big deal or not, and my team does it while doing our work.

Another useful way of looking at problems is to group them into four categories based on both preventability and the ability to correct them. The distinction between problems you can prevent, problems you cannot, the evaluation of potential problems, and your ability to deal with them affect how you manage problems.

An example of a preventable problem is a garage owner forgetting to order enough motor oil to fill his orders. On the other hand, an example of a non-preventable problem is a bakery owner dealing with rising flour prices due to years of poor wheat crops. Both examples can create problems in your business. The first means you miss opportunities to service customers until you can get the oil in stock. The increase in flour prices means that you are either going to have to raise prices or reduce your profit margins. Different ways to deal with both situations exist.

The situations with the motor oil and the wheat are fixable in the sense that there are solutions, or at least options, for how to deal with them. There are, however, other types of problems that are not fixable—or, as we call them in the law business, "irreparable." This is an important distinction to consider when dividing the potential problems into categories for management.

In the next chapter, I will begin to address the systemic nature of problems in a business due to its nature as an organization, and in doing so, I use metaphors illustrating the parallels with mechanisms and organisms. These metaphors illustrate the preventability and possible correction for problems divided into the following four groups. Here is an example of how you can categorize problems with a car:

THE FOUR TYPES OF PROBLEMS: CAR EXAMPLE

	FIXABLE	NON-FIXABLE
Preventable	Motor Oil Low	Car Totaled by a Wreck Caused by Reckless Driving
Non-Preventable	Dent from Fender Bender That Was the Other Driver's Fault	Car Totaled by Hail

Figure 3: The Four Types of Problems: Car Example

The following is an illustration of how fixable issues in an organism (specifically, the human body) can be more benign than the unfixable ones:

THE FOUR TYPES OF PROBLEMS: MEDICAL EXAMPLE

	FIXABLE	NON-FIXABLE
Preventable	Broken Arm due to Reckless Behavior	Cirrhosis of the Liver due to Drinking
Non-Preventable	Gunshot Wound to the Arm due to Assault and Battery	Massive Head Trauma due to Assault and Battery

Figure 4: The Four Types of Problems: Medical Example

Finally, the four types of problems all apply to business, too. Here is an example:

THE FOUR TYPES OF PROBLEMS: BUSINESS EXAMPLE		
	FIXABLE	**NON-FIXABLE**
Preventable	Unpaid (but Collectible) Receivable	Data Loss with No Backup
Non-Preventable	Other Party Destroys a Key Vehicle or Machine	Owner Dies in a Catastrophe

Figure 5: The Four Types of Problems: Business Example

This preventability attribute of problems directs how to deal with them. If it is preventable, it is simple enough that you seek to prevent it. Non-preventable problems have a different approach. You seek to manage these through protection, whether with insurance, backups, fail-safe procedures, or other methods. The strategies for managing non-preventable problems break down as follows:

MANAGEMENT METHODS OF THE FOUR TYPES OF PROBLEMS		
	FIXABLE	**NON-FIXABLE**
Preventable	Prevent	Prevent and Protect
Non-Preventable	Protect	Protect

Figure 6: Management Methods of the Four Types of Problems

You need to recognize the difference and consider strategies to deal with all four types of problems. This is the beginning of building your immune system. Knowing that all four problem types can occur to your company at any time, you are behooved to build in systems to avoid the non-fixable issues.

One final attribute of problems is the likelihood that they will occur. This is different from foreseeability, because it determines the percentage of likelihood that a potential problem will turn into a real one. Remember, when you set your business intentions, you planted the seeds of all your potential problems. With perfect foresight, based on years of experience and repeated mistakes, all of your problems are foreseeable. However, not all of them are likely or probable to occur.

Take, for instance, the president of a company. He is fifty years old, active, and in good health. At some point, he is going to die, because, along with taxes, death is one of the absolute certainties of life. Therefore, the company has the potential problem that its president is going to die. This is a foreseeable problem.

However, no man knows the hour of his own death. At fifty years old, our company president statistically has about thirty more years to live based on the actuarial tables and his good health. Thus, the likelihood of his passing anytime soon and leaving the company leaderless is small. Therefore, while his death is foreseeable, under the given circumstances, it is not likely to happen anytime soon.

As another example, I live in western Oklahoma right in the heart of Tornado Alley. In fact, the tornado-frequency map looks like a dartboard bull's-eye with Oklahoma City, just seventy miles to the south of my location, at its center. Every May, the tornado chasers line up on the west side of Oklahoma City and Enid to see whether they can catch a twister. Why? Because they *know* the twisters are coming, and that they are likely to occur at this time of year.

When I travel and meet people from other places and mention I live in Oklahoma, the subject of tornados frequently comes up. Usually the conversation is something like this: "Are you nuts? That has to be an insanely dangerous place to live!" Actually, it is not as dangerous as you might assume. In fact, your chances of getting caught in a tornado are slim because Oklahoma is a big place. Yes, they are incredibly dangerous. Yes, they are going to touch down every year, particularly around May. When a big tornado touches down, it is as if God took an eraser and wiped out everything in the tornado's path, but this represents a thin line on an entire sheet of paper. So, we know that tornados are foreseeable in May, but at the same time, we know that the likelihood of getting sucked up into one is slim. Still, storm shelters are a highly desirable item—thus tying in with the severity attribute of problems.

All problems are foreseeable given perfect insight into the future. However, not all problems are likely to occur. There will always be problems that slip through the defenses this book teaches you to build. Perhaps that is the core of why they call law, like medicine, a practice. However impossible or difficult, there is no sound reason to omit solid efforts to prevent problems. Furthermore, using the analysis of which problems are more likely to occur provides you with an additional advantage.

To recap—most problems we encounter have four main attributes, which, if identified, will assist us in managing them. The point of this chapter was to unravel the nature of problems so that we can apply reason to manage them. It is similar to the axiom from the Chinese military strategist Sun Tzu, "If you know your enemy and know yourself, you need not fear the outcome of a thousand battles."

Problems—or, more precisely, potential problems—are your enemy. As we go through the Preventing Stupid Method and then on to Building Your Business Immune System, the four attributes of problems will be essential to keeping your problems minimized. They are the key components of the alchemy of being ready to manage a business. The attributes form the core group of considerations that a business owner must weigh if he or she wants to prevent stupid from robbing his or her bottom line and peace of mind.

CHAPTER SUMMARY

✔ The four attributes of problems are 1) Fixable, 2) Non-fixable, 3) Preventable, and 4) Non-preventable. Problems in business are very subjective and can come in any combination of these attributes.

✔ Business owners can create a Business Problem Severity Scale to understand the problems they are facing and craft their own opinions about which problems are the most pressing.

✔ You can categorize problems in two ways: fixable versus non-fixable, and preventable versus non-preventable. By categorizing using the four problem types, business owners can create solutions to problems challenging their business's successes.

✔ Foreseeability of problems does not correlate with likelihood of occurrence. Yet prevention should be in place for all potential problems, no matter the likelihood.

Why and Where
Problems Originate

———

TOLSTOY STARTED *ANNA KARENINA* WITH, "ALL HAPPY FAMI-
lies are alike; each unhappy family is unhappy in its own way." His
point was that a family is an organization that has attributes that must
function well together to meet the needs of its members. If one or
more of these necessary parts is not present or not functioning properly, unhappiness follows, because the family is not working right.
There are close parallels to this idea in the human body, cars, and businesses. For instance, if a person's body is not functioning properly, we
deem them to be unhealthy. Likewise, if a car is running perfectly, we
call it a "well-oiled machine." The important point to grasp is that
there is a "right" way for things to run, including your business. If it
is not running smoothly, the symptoms will eventually display themselves as clearly as unhappiness does in a family, poor health does in a
body, or a flat tire does with a car.

People go into business to fulfill their dreams, make money, and
follow their passions. Frequently, they start their businesses in an ad
hoc manner, without thinking about what attributes they need for a
successful business. It is always more fun to pursue the dream than

to slow down and consider all the mundane things that are necessary to prevent a fledgling business from crashing. The susceptibility to get wrapped up in this sort of adrenaline rush is a common facet of human nature, and it is likely more rampant among enterprising citizens of America than it is in other nations. I read a snippet recently that encapsulated this, "Just remember, we put a man on the moon before we were smart enough to put wheels on our suitcases."

Most businesses begin the same way: ready to soar, but not necessarily ready to deal with the inevitability that problems of many types are going to occur. The bottom line for the new business owner is that the big idea or dream is fun and inspiring. To make their business a sustainable reality requires the organization necessary for that to happen. The new business owner, who rarely has the experience to understand the necessity of this action, frequently overlooks building in these mechanisms.

The idea of running a business correctly is complicated and requires explanation. There is no blueprint or engineering schematic. The necessary steps are not the same in every business, because every business is different, just as every family is different. Both types of organizations contain unique people, along with their idiosyncrasies, needs, and proclivities. However, as Tolstoy noted about families, there is a way to get them to "run right."

"Right" in business involves the complex art of taking complicated humans and getting them to work together as a single mechanism, which in turn produces sufficient revenue and hopefully a profit for the company. Accomplishing that is not engineering; rather, "right" in a business is a function of three things:

Practicality: Does it work? Where I live, we all knowingly joke that the best farmers can fix almost anything with duct tape and bailing wire. It might not be the prettiest fix, but generally it is cost-effective, and more importantly, it works.

Legality: A business needs to operate within the bounds of the law. If you decide not to pay your payroll tax contributions, eventually this is going to catch up with you. Likewise, if you do not operate within the bounds of the law, it is likely that you will end up in the courts, and if your conduct is egregious, it can be very expensive.

Morality: Not all legal things are moral. There is a clear difference. Just because you *can* do something legally, it does not mean that you *should* do it. Dave Ramsey comments on this in his book *Entre-Leadership*, where he states that he runs his business with the Golden Rule.[1] Treating your customers the way you would want to be treated is a rock-solid element of running your business right.

These three elements combined form what I call the "right sweet spot," based on the following diagram:

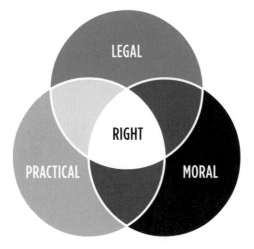

Figure 7: Three-Ring Diagram

These three elements are not always simple. They take some expertise, knowledge, and, often, professional advice. "Getting it right" is the job of every business owner or manager, and frankly, the main reason that person is so valuable to the company and well compensated is for performing this complicated balancing act.

Thus, making a business run right is an art and not a science. However, it does take discipline and the understanding of how to be rigorously critical of yourself and your business. Being haphazard will not suffice.

Returning to the idea of three rings—coincidentally, a three-ring circus is a good example of how "right" works. It takes skill, experience, and safety mechanisms. A circus run right has a variety of performers and is replete with systems both to produce entertaining spectacles and to prevent problems. The cages, for instance, are there to prevent the tigers from running uncontrolled through the crowd. Very simply, they are preventive systems, because the results of a tiger on the loose are very predictable. The trapeze artists generally have nets because the chance of missing the next bar and the attendant results of doing so are always present. If the ringmaster puts this together "right," then you have a well-run circus. Not incidentally, if you have been to the circus more than once, you will have noted that they are alike in the general sense.

What if the circus owner did not supply nets for the trapeze artists and one of them fell to their death during the show? We would say that the ringmaster did not run the circus right. In fact, we would think the owner of the circus stupid for not recognizing this. The necessary safety mechanisms were not there, and what could have been a preventable or easily manageable issue is now a very large problem. At the most basic level, that circus was not running right because the necessary and proper elements of the show were not in place.

Several analogies exist to describe situations in which an organization or an organism is not running right. However, the terms are not so clear for your business, because most business owners do not understand that their business is a series of interlocking systems, much like a body or a car. Consequently, we only have generic ways of referring to a "sick" business, such as, "The owner is running it into the ground." Regardless of the lack of terminology, when the business is not meeting its goals, it is because it is not being run right.

The key point to understand is that any sickness or functional problem within a company is merely a symptom of something not working right in the underlying systems of the business. When business owners fail to grasp the fact that their company's problems are systemic, it can cloud their judgment in seeking a solution that resolves the underlying problems in the systems. For example, a business seems to be in a perpetually critical cash-flow crunch when payroll comes due, even though the crew is constantly busy doing supposedly profitable work. The bookkeeper advises the owner of the "problem," who then spends the next day or so trying to determine which receivables are immediately collectible. Meanwhile, the owner neglects his other responsibilities.

The takeaway is that the "problem" is not the real problem. Instead, the "money-crunch issue" is just a symptom of the larger problem. Without further examination, we cannot know exactly where the systemic problem is; but based on experience, there are several reasonable options, including the following:

- The real problem could be in the business's metrics—in that they are not charging enough for the work.

- The real problem could be in the production—in that the crew is not efficiently performing its work.

- The real problem could be in the marketing, which is bringing customers who are unwilling or unable to pay the business.

When a business is not healthy, it is very similar to when a person is not healthy. There are varying degrees of illness, but when you have your health, you are free to take advantage of the opportunities around you. When you do not have your health (again, depending on the degree), tending to your malady consumes your time and energy. In business, wasting time or spending money trying to fix the symptom can consume the otherwise profitable resources of the business. Remember, problems run the gamut from being an irritant to putting you out of business. The goal is to get the systems running right and working in unison to meet your personal goals, whether that means maximizing leisure time or profits.

The initial goal of this chapter is to help business owners understand that what they consider problems are often not. Rather, they are simply symptoms of the underlying failures, or perhaps even a complete lack of knowledge regarding systems that need to be in place within their business to keep it running right. Understanding this one point gives a business owner a leg up in determining the real heart of the problems. Optimally, the action will be proactive and preventive rather than reactive and corrective. Regardless, just understanding that there is a right way for a business to run puts an owner miles ahead of the competition.

The next point is that well-run or healthy businesses have whatever systems are necessary to deal with the types of issues that naturally arise in the course of running a business. The truth is that problems *are* going to arise—stuff happens! The world keeps spinning, mistakes keep happening, and the general chaos of life is sure to present a variety of issues with which you to have to deal. This fact is foreseeable and, therefore, predictable.

This brings us to the Preventing Stupid Method, which entails building efficient systems with rigorous critical analysis to ward off foreseeable problems. Should problems arise that are indeed unpreventable, you will have the tools to resolve them.

Running a business right means the prevention of—or the ability to manage the inevitability of—problems. This is no different from what engineers do in designing the safety systems in cars or what your immune system does for your body. Cars, for instance, have windshield wipers. The reason for this is obvious—it will very likely rain at some point when you are driving your car. On a more dramatic level, cars now come with airbags because they are sometimes involved in accidents. If a car lacked these functions, you would say that it is not drivable.

However, note that these functions are incidental to the overall function of a car, which is transportation. The wipers help the driver see through the windshield in the event of foreseeable rain, while the airbags protect the passengers in the event of an unforeseeable accident. These are preventive and responsive systems built into the car, because once the "goal" of the car is established—transporting you from place to place—the manufacturing company addressed the potential problems of rain and accidents.

Our bodies are also prepared for unexpected issues. When a bacterium gets into the body, the immune system reacts to eliminate it. This action is not limited to the immune system, however. When a flesh wound occurs, the circulatory system reacts by sending platelets to coagulate and stop the bleeding. On an even more elementary level, we are blessed with eyelids so that we can blink either to wet our eyes or to keeps things out of them. If we did not have these tools, we would say that our bodies were not well designed or working right.

The human body is a common denominator with which we all are familiar, and that will help explain how a business fails. Our bodies, like businesses, are complex organisms made up of interlocking systems that must function properly for us to be healthy. In fact, the medical concept of health is synonymous with a business being well run. The concepts are so parallel that a business that has done a good job of preventing stupid has a "clean bill of health." My law firm uses the metaphor of the Business Immune System to explain how you keep your business running in prime condition.

Running right may seem like an easy task, but in reality, it is a complex term when it comes to the running of a business. It depends on practicality, legality, and morality. Getting these things in balance is the key responsibility of the owner or manager. Still, once you have your business running right, there is an art to building the Business Immune System to protect it. This art demands attention, and that is the ultimate subject of this book. Before we get to that art, however, the seven systems that exist in your business demand our attention so that you can understand exactly what it is that you are building your BIS to protect.

CHAPTER SUMMARY

✓ The "right" way to run a business is a function of practicality, legality, and morality.

✓ You can attribute all business functional problems to the failing of underlying systems.

✓ Fixing symptoms (the effect) of functional problems instead of addressing the systematic issue (the cause) is inefficient and is not conducive to business sustainability or growth.

✓ A competent business owner will build efficient systems using critical analysis to prevent foreseeable problems. Once problems arise, the business owner will have the tools necessary to resolve them.

The Seven Essential Systems of Every Business

————

THERE ARE SEVEN ESSENTIAL SYSTEMS IN EVERY BUSINESS. Some businesses have more and some have more sophisticated versions of the basic seven. The common denominator among all companies is that the seven basic systems must function for the business to survive. These seven systems function as a feedback loop that constantly feeds the business and, if done correctly, can enable a business to grow. Understanding how these systems work together is essential in grasping first how you prevent stupid from striking your business and then how you build your Business Immune System.

In every business, there are functions to accomplish. We call these functions *systems*. The seven essential systems are

- the owner;
- the personnel;
- the production (a.k.a. procedures and systems);
- the physical plant;

- the metrics;
- the marketing; and
- the sales.

Everything that goes on in a business falls into one of the seven basic systems. I mentioned that sometimes other systems are present in a business, but I ultimately view those as subsystems to these basic seven. For instance, if you run a business in a highly regulated industry or have stringent government contracting requirements, regulatory compliance or contracting might be viewed as a separate system because making sure you are within the bounds of the law is a critical function of the business. Those instances are a subfunction of production, because production is how the work gets done.

These systems also run the gamut from simple to ultrasophisticated. Marketing is a good illustration of this range. Through marketing, your business gets the right customers to your door so you can make the sale. Surprisingly, many businesses do not have a marketing plan. In fact, they ignore this function altogether. This is not just isolated to small businesses. I have clients who run multimillion-dollar businesses who do not have a dime in their marketing budget.

However, they actually are marketing, whether they know it or not. Their marketing takes place via the work they do, because their work speaks for them. This method is word-of-mouth marketing. In many ways, it is the best form of marketing, because it is free and brings in customers ready to do business. Word-of-mouth marketing is the simplest way to attract customers.

Conversely, there are businesses that rely on a full-court press marketing approach. Of course, they still hope for the free word-of-mouth marketing, but they also might employ

- radio;
- television;
- print media;
- direct mail;
- public speaking;
- social media; or
- networking events.

A business might use any combination of these or even other methods. Regardless, the purpose is the same: to fulfill the function of getting the right customers to the door and ready to engage in a sales conversation.

The systems in the business all must work together to produce profits for the owner of the business. Going back to the car metaphor, this is similar to how the engine, the brakes, the headlights, and the transmission systems combine to get the driver and passengers where they are going safely. The systems of a business similarly work together toward the common purpose, and one feeds the other in the following ways:

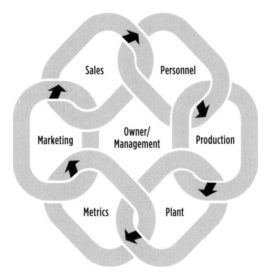

Figure 8: Circle of Business Diagram

At the center of this circle is the owner or management. The owner's function is to provide the overall vision and purpose for the business. The owner is similar to the ringmaster in the circus. All other systems depend on the goals and the competency of the owner. The owner is the brain of the organization. As businesses become more sophisticated, often a manager or a management team fulfills this purpose. Regardless of the person or persons sitting in this chair, the job of this system is to set the goals of the company and see to it that the other supporting systems are performing their functions efficiently so that the company can meet its goals.

Often when a business starts, the owner is the personnel. This was true when Hewlett and Packard started Hewlett-Packard, or Jobs and Wozniak started Apple in their respective garages. For many years, I downsized my practice so that it was just me working in my living room. While I functioned as the owner, I also functioned as the personnel. I was the one with my fingers on the keyboard turning out the letters and pleadings. I was the one taking and returning phone calls. The function of the personnel in any company is to do the work of the business, whether it is making the widgets or filing the briefs. Someone must do the job unless a machine can do it. Even then, someone must run the machine. As a business gets bigger, this system gets more complicated, not only in dealing with all the complications of having employees but also in making sure the business is following labor laws. The purpose of the personnel system is to ensure there are enough qualified, trained people to handle the work that sales bring into the business.

Sales drives the need for personnel, and the team needs an organized, reliable way of doing the work. The production system is how the company produces the product. Another way of looking at this is to consider production as a factory. A factory is not necessarily a *physical plant*. Instead, production—or "factory"—is *how* the business does its work. Production encapsulates the methods that personnel uses to accomplish the work of the business.

If your business is a plumbing company, then your plant is out in the field. It is a process of fixing leaks, clearing clogs, running new lines, and so forth. All these jobs require certain skills. These skills, plus experience, are all a part of the system of how the business works. For instance, if you are plumbing a new house, a procedure exists for how to hook up the water. A procedure also exists for how to hook the sinks up to water, and a slightly different one exists for the sewer. Processes also exist for installing the drainage system. The procedures required to accomplish this work make up the production system.

The example of a plumbing company is a good one to illustrate the range of physical plants that a business can have. I know plumbers who operate right out of their trucks. They most likely have a small home office for billing and record keeping, but otherwise their shop is on the road. The physical plant is wherever they do their work. Some businesses do not require dedicated real estate to fill this function. Others are real estate–intensive.

Depending on the type of work, the physical plant can function in a variety of ways. My law firm represents a trucking company. Obviously, a good deal of its work is hauling goods from place to place. In that sense, the real estate demands are nonexistent. However, maintenance, repairs, dispatching, safety, sales, human resources, and a litany of other functions within the company do require terminals and offices to perform this work. Similarly, my law firm maintains its main office in Enid. The nature of our work is such that a good deal of it can be performed anywhere. Nearly half of the attorneys on my team are in places as far away as South Carolina. In short, the physical plant can fulfill the needs of the business in many ways.

With the work in progress, a business needs to plan, measure, manage, and receive payment. These and other aspects of your business are the functions of the metrics system. Metrics makes sure that the other systems are performing their overall functions of bringing in and producing paying work. One job of this system is measuring productivity of the personnel. In service businesses, keeping track of revenue-producing hours is the most common measure. Other businesses measure productivity by the units produced, miles driven, or square feet of roofing installed.

Productivity is just one part of the metrics system. Another is the performance of the business in relation to the goals set by the owner. Thus, budgeting is part of the metrics system. By budgeting, I do not mean simply establishing a budget, but also checking the business's performance in relation to the budget and assessing any variances from it.

Metrics function like a car's dashboard. The numbers it produces let the owner, manager, and personnel know about the business's performance. It is like the speedometer, tachometer, gas gauge, and the other instruments on the dash. The function of metrics is to provide information to the other systems, which, when working together, advance toward the overall goal of profits. If not, the metrics will tell the owner where the problem is so it can be resolved.

These profits, however, will never materialize without the customers. The marketing system brings customers to the sales table. Marketers refer to this as a funnel. This process separates people who need your goods and services from those who do not. Another function of marketing is vetting the potential customers to determine their ability to pay for your products or services.

As I mentioned earlier, marketing systems come in a variety of different strategies. Six of the most common are

- direct contract with existing customers;
- networking and referral building;
- public speaking;
- writing and publicity;
- promotional events; and
- advertising.

As I stated earlier, some businesses rely merely on word-of-mouth marketing, which is in the category of direct contact with existing customers. Typically, however, businesses employ a mixture (or possibly all) of the above methods to build their marketing system.

As an example, my law firm maintains close contact with our existing customers. We also actively network with other law firms engaged in noncompetitive legal work, insurance firms, accounting firms, and other businesses to build our network. Several members of my firm take on speaking engagements, and this book clearly falls in the writing category. We also host dinners and parties at the firm to cement our relationships with existing clients and to build our referral network. As my firm began to outgrow our existing marketing efforts, we instituted advertising using social media. These marketing systems have the function of bringing the right customers to our firm.

Once you identify potential customers who meet your criteria, including booking new work for existing customers, you need to close the sale. I have a client who does commercial roofing jobs. He always works for the same general contractors. His sales system is a function of his marketing. His customers already trust him and want him to do the job because he does it right. His sales system is just about pricing the jobs fairly within the going market rates. He can probably even demand a slight premium due to the reliability of his work and the trusting relationship that he has with the general contractors.

We have some customers with whom my firm has similar relationships. One day, a new lawyer to my firm was having trouble understanding the ongoing relationship and pricing that the firm had with an established client. So I taught her about these relationships. I tossed an L.L.Bean polo shirt on her desk and told her that this was our firm in relation to the client. This confused her, so I explained that I always buy my polos from L.L.Bean because I know they are good quality and they are easy for me to get online. I can get something of lesser quality at JCPenney for considerably less money, but I prefer the better quality and reliability of L.L.Bean, and I am willing to pay for it. Then I explained that our client could get some of the services we provide for him done more cheaply by other firms. However, his time is exceptionally valuable, and it is worth it to him to have our firm, which he respects and trusts, handle all his legal needs rather than shop out his tasks piecemeal. This saves him time and hassle, so our firm providing him with a one-stop shop is beneficial to him. Now she understands that a good proportion of our sales work this way.

Of course, not all sales systems work because of a trust relationship. I have a friend who runs a law firm in Gillette, Wyoming, specializing in DUI defense. She astutely markets her firm with the slogan "Everyone deserves a dignified DUI defense." This attracts clients and speaks to the people ashamed of their situations. The vast majority of her clients are good citizens caught making a one-time mistake. They are apprehensive and are not experienced in hiring a criminal defense lawyer. This business demands an entirely different sales system to present the value proposition to the potential client.

Because her firm does not have long-term clients, her sales systems are different from my firm's sales systems, at least concerning our long-standing client base. It is, however, like our sales system in relation to how we bring in our new clients. We must be able to demonstrate to them how we can provide value to protect their time, money, or reputations. Sales systems, like nearly all the other systems, range from elementary to complex. No exact science exists about making sales, but legal, moral, and practical values should govern a business's sales practices. Your sales system must adhere to the goals of the business, because, again, the sales system feeds the need for the personnel system, and from there the entire business functions around the wheel of systems.

Your business contains systems that perform functions. The complexity or sophistication of these systems depends on the nature of, and the goals for, the business. Ultimately, the objective is to get the systems all working together to create a feedback loop that earns the profit the owner's goals require. A healthy business that has all seven basic systems working right is a business that is very valuable and a pleasure to run. However, when one or more of the systems is not performing its necessary function, this sick business is a headache at best and a heartbreak at worst. Over time, what separates a successful business from a sick business is not luck. Just as a body needs its immune system, so too does a business. A Business Immune System protects the other systems from potential illness and helps resolve the issues causing problems. Business owners often miss this critical distinction, and it could cost them dearly.

CHAPTER SUMMARY

✔ For a business to run smoothly, each of the seven systems must function properly. These include the owner, the personnel, the production, the physical plant, the metrics, the marketing, and the sales.

✓ Six of the systems revolve around the owner, the center of the circle of business.

✓ Although the systems may present differently for every type of business, each system exists in a business and is important to stability and success.

✓ The objective is to create a business where all systems work together in a feedback loop that makes the profit the owner's goals require.

The Eighth System

"THE BEST DEFENSE IS A GOOD OFFENSE." THE MILITARY CALLS this the strategic offensive principle. While this may be a useful strategy in war, it is ineffective in the business world. Rather, the best defense is a *good defense* accomplished efficiently without interfering with the business's overall goals. This means it must work within all seven systems concurrently. Unfortunately, many business owners either neglect or do not understand this fact.

I will concede that business has some similarities to war or sports. When you get that big account or collect on that big job, phrases such as "took their market" or "scored a touchdown" convey the sense of excitement that comes from winning. Business can be fun; in fact, it should be. You could be scoring "points" by making dollars. Being the one who scores the goal is an awesome feeling. However, this is not a game; your business is real life. Whether you can pay the mortgage or send your kids to college depends entirely on you.

Most businesses are not straight-up conflicts, such as war, or simple competitions, such as sports games. I agree that when a product or service commoditizes, the strategic offensive principle tends to apply more readily. For instance, if you are selling gasoline at an intersection with four gas stations on it, you really do need to be offensive with your pricing. Alternatively, if you are the only filling station on a long stretch of desert highway, your main goal is to prevent the stupid mistake of letting your tanks run out of gas.

Most businesses ply their wares or services based on a particular specialization or a trust relationship. People usually choose a clothing store because they like what the store typically carries, even if the store is a bit more expensive than other places in town. Skilled trades and many other businesses work the same way. Likewise, in the law business—except for things like misdemeanors and no-asset divorces—people seek out counsel that they trust and believe will add value to their goals. Having a smoothly running business that enables the owner or manager to deliver their goods or services on time without problems or distractions is important.

Offense is critically important to success in business. Having goals and taking steps to reach them is what leads to business growth and, in many cases, the survival of the business. You also need to address the defensive parts of your business. I want to stress again the idea that you do not run a business on *just* preventing stupid, but you *really* do not run a business without doing it. That means you must know how to protect your end of the operations.

One day my pastor, Dan Barrick, admonished the congregation about all the messes they were making in their lives. He delivered a line that stuck with me ever since, "You don't have to be smart; just don't be stupid." The gravity of those words worked its way through my mind and into all the predicaments that I routinely must fix for my clients. The common denominator was, of course, stupid mistakes. Thinking back, I realize I could have easily prevented the vast majority of my clients' draining problems.

A good example is a recent wholesale business that we helped set up. The owners wanted to go with a generic name that was, frankly, boring and forgettable. These were smart operators in the underlying trade, but they had never been involved in the wholesale business. Little thought had gone into how to reach their customers. Their target customer market was local tradesmen, and my team identified the competitive advantage that this business could achieve with a good website, a memorable name, and an online inventory.

Together we developed a list of solid names for the business and then did the research to determine the domain names available for use. We chose a name that met both requirements (memorable and available). We got the company started on a good footing, ready to implement the strategy. We did this in part by avoiding the problem that a bad name can cause a business. In addition, we ensured that we had ownership of the domain, because without it our strategy was pointless. Before the business even began to operate, we built in the protection of the marketing system.

Another potential problem involves your team getting complacent in how they perform the work of your business. Your company's training procedure for its employees may be spectacular. You can have a dedicated training facility and fly the new employees in from all over the country for rigorous instruction before you ever let them start their work. You can take all the right steps to make sure all the necessary skill sets are in place. As well you should, because this is how you build a rock-solid company.

However, most work is repetitious and routine. An employee gets into a groove doing the same thing day after day. They may even make the same round-robin trip or do the same task several times a day. On the one hand, it is easy work. First, the employees check the equipment, and then they get to work. They are well-trained professionals who know their jobs.

To most business owners this may seem like an ideal situation, and it almost is. The problem is that it is exactly this sort of repetitive work where the stupidest, most preventable errors can happen. It even happens to the most highly trained professionals in the world. Surgical teams, for instance, leave sponges in patients all the time when they do not follow the checklist to make sure every little step is done right. Pilots have checklists as well. In nearly every business the risks can become commonplace, and the dangers of the job can get lost in the routine.

Stupid mistakes happen when human error takes over. Due to boredom, fatigue, or a litany of other issues, something happens and you suddenly—and sometimes disastrously—have a problem on your hands. These mistakes happen. One of the remedies that can prevent this type of situation is to implement checklists that break up the routine and lead to spot checks to keep your workers on task.

This is one way to mount a good defense. Checklists allow you to prevent the ineptitude of interrupted production and the extra operational costs required to correct it. It also prevents management from being distracted, so they can stay focused on their real goal: finding new customers and closing deals. Address the situation with the truism "A mistake made more than once is a decision," and avoid slipping into complacency with the decision that "these things are going to happen."

It is incumbent on management to take back the power to change the company's policy and make the decision that this situation will not happen again. With the right management techniques (ensuring repetitive work correctly executed by using checklists), you can ferret out this ineptitude, thereby improving your bottom line.

Putting defenses like this in place does not take the control away from the management. Instead, it frees them up to assert their efforts on business development rather than fixing the business. I stress control because it is one of the two most common issues business owners and their managers worry about, rather than where they should be putting their energy: on creating good defenses. They want hands-on control, when the more passive measures often serve them better. The truth is, a good defense adds to your control.

The other issue that prevents business owners from establishing good defenses is the satisfaction they derive in being the hero. Frankly, many business owners are addicted to the adrenaline pump of rushing in to fix the problem, thereby showing off their skills. The payoff for them is the immediate rush of gratitude by employees or customers.

What I suggest is that you ask yourself what you can do to prevent stupid mistakes from ruining your business. This is thinking proactively. Unfortunately, most business owners tend to think of fixing the problem that now exists, which is a reactive thought process. Changing your thinking from reactive to proactive will take the burden of being the hero off your shoulders. You do not really want to be the hero anyway. Most of the "hero work" done in a business is fixing preventable problems the owner allowed to happen in the first place.

Talent is a curse. Those with it tend to rely on it to pull themselves through tough times without relying on the slow and steady steps that would otherwise get them where they want to go. Think back to the tortoise and the hare. The point of the story is just that: slow and steady wins the race.

To combat this curse, I stress to my clients the importance of "rhythm and bass." Think about it when you are driving down the road listening to a song. The foundation of the music is not the singer or the guitar player. What makes the music work is the rhythm section—the drummer with the tight beat, and the solid bass that keeps the music moving along.

Business is the same. You have to play that rhythm and bass every day if you want to make that song a hit. Winners know that consistency over time is the key to success. Just like the tortoise winning the race, what counts is doing your job consistently, steadily, and correctly—and then getting your employees to do the same. On one hand, you are responsible for all of this on the offensive side of your business; but if you really want your business to succeed, you need that eighth system protecting the rest.

It is easy to overlook the rhythm and bass of defense for several reasons, primarily because people go into business to do or produce something they know. Most of the time, preventing stupid mistakes is not in their skill set. They start their businesses to do what they love to do and make money at it; consequently, many business owners neglect to update the protections for their business, even those that they already have in place. In fact, many business owners never give a moment of thought to preventing stupid mistakes. Nine times out of ten, that attitude translates into a recipe for failure.

In this chapter, my goal has been to illustrate both offense and defense in order to show you how important they are for your business.

They are the foundation for building a responsible, life-changing business. Chances are, if you are just starting out in your own business, you need to learn these skills. If you are already running your own business, you most likely have made many mistakes and learned your lessons the hard way. Unfortunately, you still face the danger of becoming complacent. Businesses change and grow, so you always need to implement new ways to protect them. Not doing so will almost certainly cost you dearly. The next chapter addresses the three questions you need to learn to prevent stupid mistakes, because these questions are the foundation of building your BIS. Learning how to answer these questions and apply them to your business will help you move fast and with confidence to improve both your business and your life.

CHAPTER SUMMARY

✓ More important than addressing business competitors is acting as a trusted and loved business for clients. This only happens through the efficient work performed by a company that is distraction-free due to the problem-prevention measures in place.

✓ Managers must utilize checklists and policies, which not only prevent employee mistakes but also free managers from putting out fires or completing tasks meant for lower-level employees.

✓ Business owners often want to be the hero by fixing pressing mistakes. Proactive measures can prevent the mistakes from happening and free the owner from the hero mentality.

✓ While the talent of a business owner has merit, the ability to do the job consistently, steadily, and correctly is key.

The Preventing Stupid Method

BEFORE YOU CAN BUILD YOUR BUSINESS IMMUNE SYSTEM, you need to identify what type of potential problems you may encounter. Therefore, the Preventing Stupid Method is the first step in the two-step process to establish your Business Immune System. This first step is the process of identifying and categorizing. I call this process Preventing Stupid because it is stupid to allow your potential problems to develop into real-life issues, and once you know the right questions to ask, it is really rather simple to identify them. The crux of being efficiently able to accomplish this task is to ask yourself three questions pertaining to the likeliness of (1) catastrophes, (2) your own ignorance, and (3) your team's ineptitude as they relate to the systems in your business.

Once you recognize and evaluate the threats, you can begin to design your Business Immune System to prevent or respond to them. Understanding the nature of problems and the systemic nature of your business becomes critical when you examine your business to evaluate its existing problems and determine which of the potential problems are most likely to surface. Chapter 3 introduced the origin of problems in the systems of your business. There, I stressed the systemic nature of business but only addressed the question of where the problems might come from. This is the foundation of understanding how to manage your potential problems proactively rather than tackling them reactively.

For instance, if you have an unemployment claim, you now can recognize there is an issue in your personnel system, and you can correct the situation by making the necessary adjustments. Similarly, a large, uncollected account receivable is a problem in your sales, marketing, or metrics systems. This bird's-eye view of your business is an essential step in examining the reasons potential problems can arise and helps you identify them before they bloom into serious issues.

The question of "where" is obviously not the only question you need to ask. It is, however, the first one that you need to resolve, because answering all the other important questions depends on your understanding that your business problems are a function of your systems not working correctly. This chapter introduces the critical "why" and "how" questions. These questions delve into the reasons that propel a business's problems. They reveal the cause behind a particular problem arising from the myriad of potential issues. Causes are different from origins; they are instead answers to different questions. Remember, when you set your business goals, you plant the seeds of all your future business problems. In fact, they are two sides of the same coin.

Let us focus on the human systems behind a business. Human will and rational thought control these systems. As the business owner, you are the head and you have ultimate control of the systems of your business. This includes your Business Immune System. It is your responsibility to establish and maintain these systems. You must also safeguard them from the potential problems you created when you set your goals at the outset of forming your company.

Because a business is a complex human system that you oversee, *you* are the answer to the "why" and "how" of problem development. You started the business. You set it in motion. You created the goals. Then you failed along the way to establish and maintain your business's systems. You are the moving force behind why potential problems blossom into real-time disasters, because you failed to appropriately prepare for or manage them. The vast majority of the problems that you, as a business owner, face in your business are your own fault.

When you started this book, you probably breezed past that line. Now I hope you pause and see not only its truth and significance but also the freedom that accepting it gives you. If things are your fault, if you failed, then you can change. As Henry Ford put it, "Failure is simply the opportunity to begin again, this time more intelligently."[1] You can improve, and you can learn how to build your business the right way. No one does it right the first time, the second, or the third. The goal is to get better each time. The goal is to get your Business Immune System stronger every day. As you get smarter and more experienced, that is exactly what should be happening. There is an art to running a successful business, and with time, you will improve.

Fortunately, building this skill set is achievable. The good news is that there are only three reasons you can fail. The simplicity of examining your business based on these questions is why I refer to the process as Preventing Stupid. Again, failure results from only these three reasons:

- You failed to prepare for foreseeable catastrophes.
- You remained ignorant about the jobs of your systems.
- You were inept at implementing the ongoing work of your business.

These are the three main responsibilities of a business owner. Failures that strike a business come in these three forms. Each failure type has a method of resolution, thereby preventing what should be minor hassles from becoming massive, company-wide threats.

Business owners and managers who routinely and systematically address these three questions generally avoid the stupid mistakes that would otherwise impede a business's performance. Any unforced stupid error that can occur in your business will fall into one of these three categories. In effect, these categories frame the three questions that you—or your general counsel—constantly need to ask about your business. If you can put all those worrying ideas into one of three categories, you can clear your mind to begin to deal with them in an organized and effective manner; consequently, running your business becomes infinitely easier.

These problems are your enemies, and if you know your enemy, you need not fear the outcome of the battle, because you will win, or, at the very least, be prepared to deal with what happens. Dealing with a problem you can foresee is considerably easier than one that comes unexpectedly.

If you do not adequately perform these duties, you are going to have a whole host of problems, and there is a good chance your business life is going to be reactive, because your business is going to be sick. The following questions outline the three reasons for business failure:

- What are the foreseeable disasters that can strike my business?
- What particular skills or knowledge do my team and I need to run the business effectively?
- What systems and procedures do we need in order to ensure that the work is executed efficiently, safely, and correctly the first time?

Failures are going to happen to your business. You are going to suffer accidents, setbacks, and mistakes. You cannot prevent all of them, but what you can do is

- minimize the number of them; and
- minimize the deleterious effects these failures have on your business.

I maintain that these two goals are paramount in your role as the business's manager—perhaps even more important than your role of strategizing and providing leadership for your organization. If you are spending nine times the effort fixing the inevitable-but-preventable problems, then you were not prepared.

These are your basic obligations to yourself and your family as a business owner. They are the keys to understanding the obstacles to your goals. They open the doors to understanding the threats to your success. Getting clear answers to these questions provides the foundation for building your BIS, because the answers to these questions outline the potential problems that the BIS intends to prevent (or to prepare you to be ready to resolve). I stressed early on that my definition of stupid is simply not building these protections into your system. All three of these reasons are controllable, and a quick examination of them will illustrate why.

Catastrophes are the natural and man-made disasters that hinder your goals. They generally originate outside your business. Sometimes they derive from forces of nature, such as fire, flood, tornado, or hurricane. Another source is market fluctuations. Here in western Oklahoma, for instance, a considerable number of the companies depend on oil production for their livelihood. In 2014, the oil price crashed from $120 per barrel to below $30. This was a catastrophe for those who did not see it coming. However, it was not a catastrophe for our clients, because we saw it coming and helped them prepare for it.

At other times, catastrophes can come from people or companies outside your own. This may be the competition. It could be a disgruntled former employee or unhappy customer deciding to disparage your company on the internet. The common thread is that all of these are outside your ability to control. You cannot control the forces of nature or the marketplace. The competition and other random people have free will. Therefore, the only thing you can do in the face of catastrophes is to anticipate their likelihood and prepare for them. Assessing this is what we discussed in chapter 2. Again, this is not as hard as it initially seems. It does take some effort, and you will get better at it with introspection, education, and experience. That process is building your Business Immune System, and it is the subject of the next chapter.

The one notable exception to the "external rule" regarding catastrophes is your mental and physical health. As the head of the nervous system of your business (a.k.a. the brain), if you die or lose your sanity, it will be a major catastrophe for your company, unless you have prepared for it. I face this potential disaster all the time with clients who have not attended to the very real likelihood that at some undetermined time, they are going to depart from this world, or, possibly, become incapacitated. Rarely does one receive notice for this type of catastrophe.

Returning to one of the initial principles of this book, when you set your goals, you establish your company's potential problems. This narrows down the list of potential catastrophes that can develop. Likewise, if you thoughtfully consider things like your market, the competition, and our natural environment, the list gets smaller still. Then, finally, there is you and your health to consider. Except for the owner's health, all these other issues are external forces that can sneak through your BIS and impede your company's progress. The key to preventing this is sound foresight coupled with preparation and insurance.

Ignorance, on the other hand, is squarely on your shoulders, because it is your responsibility to know how to run your business. This is a reason for failure because it covers a lack of knowledge regarding your business. This can strike either the management or the operations side of your business; consequently, it applies to both you and your employees. You fix this problem with education, such as an ongoing crash course in business management or the technical aspects of the work. Whether you are a skilled tradesman running a service company or a merchant running the corner quick shop, your business requires a remarkable number of skills that you probably do not have. However, you can learn them or hire someone who does have them.

The trick is recognizing what you do not know. The question to ask yourself continuously is, "What particular skills or knowledge do my team and I need in order to effectively run the business?" It is not a perfect science. It is also a moving target, because as your company grows or changes, you will have new things to learn and new skills to master. This is where outside firms from the legal, consulting, accounting, human resources, or marketing worlds can step in to provide valuable advice or assistance. In cooperation with you, they help you be rigorously critical about addressing the ignorance in your company's personnel.

There is no shame in this ignorance. The person with the master's in business administration does not necessarily understand the practical skill set and market secrets that are the backbone of your business. However, the converse is true for you, because you devoted your life to becoming a pro at what you do rather than the intricacies of business management. The good news is you can take that crash course. It is not very hard, because you don't have to be smart; just don't be stupid. Again, stupid is neglecting to repeatedly ask yourself the tough questions about what you and your team need to know but don't.

Ineptitude is different from ignorance because it covers things that you and your employees actually know but screw up anyway. The fixes here are things like systems, checklists, and routines. The goal is to minimize, or better yet prevent, the element of human error, which is completely avoidable using sound management. On one hand, this is the most tedious part of a business owner's job, but on the other, it is the most liberating when done correctly. Once you get your systems, checklists, and routines in place for your employees, you should never have to do those tasks again. Instead, your job becomes spot-checking their work and spending the rest of your time growing the business.

Ineptitude is also one of the most common impediments to a business's growth because the fear of it keeps the owner from delegating work to subordinates. This happens when an owner recognizes the complexity of the job and does not want to let go of the work because he or she is afraid that no one else can do it correctly. More often than not, the owner does not know how to direct the work of the employees, even after their training.

I have a friend who has an agricultural spraying business. Although spraying is relatively easy work, if you accidentally spray the wrong field, it can be a very costly mistake. You can kill an entire crop, and the accidental part does not matter under the law. A claim against a spraying company for applying chemicals to the wrong crop falls under strict liability—so the spraying company pays for the loss even if it is an accident. I know this may sound like a remote possibility; but when you live in farm country, where the fields are all half-mile-by-half-mile squares, the fields all start to look alike. It can and does happen. My friend insists on doing all his jobs himself for fear of ineptitude on the part of his employees. We have discussed options for using global positioning system controls coupled with a checklist to guard against mistakes, but fear of ineptitude still paralyzes him.

Later in this book, I will illustrate with three examples how these three categories of failure threaten a business's success. For now, however, I want to turn your attention toward prioritizing the potential problems. This takes us back to chapter 2 and the attributes of problems. It is important to determine the potential severity, the preventability, and the likelihood of occurrence. Earlier I referred to this as an alchemy, meaning this could be a complicated and uncertain affair. In fact, you are almost sure to get your prioritization incorrect. This does not matter; you will get better over time.

Please note that I use the words "avoid the *stupid* mistakes" and not the words "avoid the pitfalls." This choice of words is intentional. Catastrophes, ignorance, and ineptitude are going to happen, but they do not have to be the stupid kind. Business owners are not going to catch everything, but they can stop the stupid unforced errors. These errors stem from a mindset that fails to engage in the reality of running a business. The good news is that as an owner grows in experience, avoiding the stupid mistakes gets easier, even as the business grows.

A sound Business Immune System is the ultimate goal of this process. Understanding why and how you can fail in building and maintaining your BIS is how you grasp the reasons you can fail.

The core of the Preventing Stupid Method is to ask the three crucial questions and then apply them to the seven working parts of your business. Vulnerabilities in your business are easy to control because they revolve around the three questions about catastrophes, ignorance, and ineptitude. Remember, all failures in business fall into one of these three categories, and there are really only three ways to fail. Asking yourself the questions about these categories provides the basis for building your BIS, because these questions map out your weaknesses. Returning to Sun Tzu's work—the questions let you know your enemy in your potential problems, and you know yourself, so you do not have to fear the outcome of the battle because with these tools, you will win the war of business success.

CHAPTER SUMMARY

- ✓ Preventing stupid begins with recognizing and evaluating threats to your business.

- ✓ Once a business owner recognizes threats, he or she must create a Business Immune System Report to recognize shortcomings in addressing current and potential problems.

- ✓ Origins of business failure are threefold: you failed to prepare for predictable catastrophes, you were ignorant about the jobs of systems, and you were inept at understanding the ongoing work of your business.

- ✓ Failure is inevitable, but you can minimize the number of failures and lessen their severity if you, as business owner, foresee disaster and invest in skills to run the business effectively.

- ✓ Catastrophes come from three origins: forces of nature, the marketplace, and external sources (competition or ordinary people). Preparation for and prevention of catastrophe puts a business on the road to success.

- ✓ A successful business owner will not remain ignorant, but instead educate himself or herself on how to manage a business adequately.

- ✓ Business owners must understand how to correctly complete each task within the business and create checklists for those tasks and then delegate the tasks to subordinates. The business owner can then focus on business growth.

Building Your
Business Immune System

———

I SPECIFICALLY CHOSE THE WORD "BUILDING" TO CONVEY THE idea of constructing your BIS. It takes work, it takes time, and it takes design. Your BIS does not just spring into existence fully formed and ready to ward off or fix all your problems. Like all the other systems of your business, it takes effort, attention, and ongoing maintenance.

The construction process started with the Preventing Stupid Method. That process helped you identify and categorize the potential and existing problems in your business. Knowing what you must deal with is one thing. Knowing how to handle your problems is another thing entirely. The fundamental tool that you need to build your BIS is the right attitude. Simply stated, the right mindset is one of confidence that you can and will build it. I realize that may sound like an oversimplification; but that is where many business owners lose their momentum, stall out, and join the ranks of failures or mediocrities. Henry Ford was correct when he stated, "Whether you think you can, or you think you can't—you're right."

Once you have your BIS Report completed, you must decide which weakness you tackle first. If you identified numerous potential and existing problems, you probably recognized the most serious ones. Note that I said "most," because as you get more experienced at preventing stupid, you will get even more rigorous and critical in your evaluation process.

The question is one of priorities. It is a very difficult process to decide what problem to address first. Absent any imminent, business-threatening issues, my default position is to start with the owner. There are two main reasons for this approach. First is the principle that the business is never bigger than the ideas in the owner's head. The owner must be the brain making sure the other systems are functioning right. The second reason I tend to start with the owners is to free up their brain capacities to deal with issues outside of themselves and their families, so they can get on with running the business. Getting the owner functioning right is often the fundamental improvement that moves all others.

As a matter of admission, when I first analyzed my firm using this method, I was critical of my management of the firm. In the catastrophe column, I realized that I did not have a succession plan in place. Yes, I had a last will and testament leaving everything to my wife and kids, but because none of them has a law degree, by law they cannot own a law firm. My whole point of building the firm, beyond providing for us during my lifetime, was to leave a business for them. That really made me think, and so in conjunction with my lifelong friend, who also has a license to practice law, we worked out a reasonable accommodation to this problem.

Similarly, in the ignorance column I noted a batch of issues—not only in business management but also in the technical work of the firm—that I recognized I needed to understand better. The technical side of the firm was mostly due to the firm's growth. There is a reason that they call it a law "practice," because there never seems to be an end to the things you learn. Frankly, every business is this way. Nevertheless, I was able to identify and plan for the things I knew I needed to learn. Then there was the ineptitude column. While there is little to be ashamed about with ignorance, when you know how to do your job right and are not doing it, that is another thing altogether. My analysis enlightened me on the reasons I like to start with the owner. I recognized that I was not playing rhythm and bass in keeping track of the firm's metrics. I had attorneys not meeting their billing quotas. I had attorneys taking cases that increased receivables we could never collect. I knew better than this. I had simply failed to do my job of managing the firm. The main people suffering for it were my family and me, because all the members of the firm received a salary, but my profit for their work (or lack thereof) never materialized. Taking care of these issues made all the difference, not only in freeing my brain space to deal with other issues but also in expanding my thinking to develop the skills I needed.

Smart managers realize they make stupid mistakes every day. One of my favorite lines that Harvey Mackay repeatedly states in his business-advice classic *Swim with the Sharks Without Being Eaten Alive* is, "I can't believe how stupid I was just two weeks ago."[1] Similarly, Jim Collins titled the fourth chapter of *Good to Great* "Confront the Brutal Facts." Jim Collins rightly asserted that a business climate where one hears and listens to the truth is a critical component of peak business performance.[2] We all need regular course corrections. The smart ones recognize this and stay attuned to critically thinking about where and how they are making unforced errors.

Back to the main point, the default first priority is the owner because he is the puppet master of the whole operation. All the other systems depend on this one working right. From there the prioritization depends on a complicated qualitative analysis. I am again referring to the alchemy I touched on in chapter 2. In that chapter, I identified several attributes of problems. This is the point where understanding these attributes becomes critically relevant. How a given potential or existent problem might affect the business is part of the consideration, as is the ease of preventing or fixing the problem.

Here is an example of how to make such a decision: I have a client who runs a construction business. When we first started working with him, he was a general contractor who took all sorts of odd jobs, from small home repairs to commercial construction, up to a million-dollar project here and there. This business demanded a wide variety of skill sets among his employees and subcontractors. It also required his forty years of expertise in the business to ensure that he consistently bid jobs profitably.

While he loved the work and the challenge of using his considerable skills, he was now in his sixties, and he wanted to simplify the business to include only his most profitable line of services—polymer concrete refinishing. The new products on the market made this an optimal choice, as did the requirements of expensive tools that he could afford but that many others could not. With that new goal in motion, this existing business now had a completely new set of issues.

In resetting the goals of the business, he also upended the status of his BIS. I sat down with him and we worked through the new potential and existing problems. For the sake of our discussion, here is the BISR that I put together for him:

	CATASTROPHE	IGNORANCE	INEPTITUDE
Management	A	D	A
Personnel	F	C	C
Production	A	A	A
Plant	A	A	A
Metrics	A	C	A
Marketing	A	D	A
Sales	A	C	A

Figure 9: BISR Sample 1

We evaluated my findings and agreed they were correct. This exercise helped establish the priorities for us to work on, starting with the lowest grades. Here are his reasons for the grades below a C:

1:2 Ignorance in Management: My client is a seasoned businessperson and particularly so in the construction trades. However, this new venture required several new skill sets that he needed to manage. He now had only one line of business, and that required building a dedicated crew. Previously, he could easily replace contractors if he lost one, so this new business model demanded a much different level of business leadership. Building this new book of business presented challenges in getting customers and making sure that the work lived up to his reputation. You will note how the weaknesses in this system spill over into some of the other low grades.

2:1 Catastrophe in Personnel: The personnel issues are now critical. While this new business is more complicated than traditional flooring methods, once the team learns the trade, they can set up their own business or go work for any competitor that might surface. In Oklahoma, noncompete clauses are very difficult to enforce because the statute allows a very limited scope. This business is not one with repeat customers, because once the contractor installs a floor, it will not need replacing for years. Therefore, the use of nonsolicitation clauses, which are easily enforceable, does not afford much protection. Very simply the change in the business direction made it highly susceptible to a catastrophic mutiny of personnel.

6:2 Ignorance in Marketing: Prior to changing the structure of the business, the owner ran a fairly successful marketing campaign relying on radio, print, and local television advertisements to attract a wide range of customers. Now the shift of the business from being a general construction and repair company to a custom, one-line workshop made all the prior marketing irrelevant. The situation involved dropping years of successful marketing because we had yet to identify the business's target customer. The flooring was usable for either inside or outside. It could be for residential or commercial use. At this point, it was not clear which one of these alternatives offered the business the best profit margins and the opportunity to garner enough work to meet the goals.

In essence, we created a potential and existing problem analysis based on the severity, probability, and preventability factors. To ignore any of these three issues could have easily defeated the business's objectives, and that would have been stupid. However, we developed strategies to address each of them. For instance, we put together a highly attractive compensation package for the key personnel in the new line of business. It encouraged them to do quality work and rewarded their marketing and selling efforts by adding a commission structure to their regular salaries. To the owner's benefit, a large part of improving this system was a result of developing a solution to the personnel issues. Another combined fix was careful tracking of the profitability of the jobs by categories to determine whether residential or commercial jobs were preferable. This categorization would also extend well into the future as he tracked the differential in maintenance and repair expenses between interior and exterior jobs.

This business was going through a renovation. In many ways, this kind of scenario is more difficult than building from scratch. It is not unlike living in a house while you are remodeling it. All the dust, noise, and reworking disrupt your daily routine. I have experienced both a house and a business remodel, and I know how difficult they can be. Although starting a business from the ground up generally involves many challenges, they are rarely of the same type. When you are starting out, your need for capital is quite different than when you are trying to maintain the cash flow necessary for an existing business while you transition to the new enterprise.

To illustrate the point, let's say you want to start a new business doing bookkeeping. This is your first business of your own, but you know the trade, having worked as a bookkeeper for a medium-sized local business for several years. Your goal is to get the business to half a million dollars a year. Your initial BISR would probably look something like this, depending on the other skill sets that you bring to the table:

	CATASTROPHE	IGNORANCE	INEPTITUDE
Management	F	F	A
Personnel	A	F	A
Production	C	F	A
Plant	C	C	A
Metrics	C	C	A
Marketing	C	F	A
Sales	C	F	A

Figure 10: BISR Sample 2

First, notice all the As in the Ineptitude column. This is not because you, as the owner and potential team, are super skilled and perform your jobs correctly and on time. Instead, it is because at this stage of the business, you have no experience running your company; therefore, the issues shift over to the Ignorance column. As the business becomes more mature, ineptitude becomes a more common problem.

Next, you will note the F in the Catastrophe: Management box. This is because the business starts as wholly dependent on you, the owner. Until you build a solid team or purchase some substantial life insurance, the entire operation is vulnerable to anything, including disability or even death. Depending on your age and health, this might not be very likely; however, due to the severity of the impact on the company, this area of the owner system deserves some attention.

Then there is the Ignorance column, replete with failing grades. This is because as the business owner, you are new to owning your operation. You have a lot to learn, and this should not come as a surprise. Once you know the skill sets required in your business, it begins to get easier. This phenomenon is exactly why wealthy businesspeople tend to get wealthier; they have already learned a great deal, primarily by making stupid mistakes!

As our new business owner, you do not have to suffer through a constant series of unforced errors. The goal is to use foresight to determine what skills you need to develop and then to go about attaining them. This is the core part of building your BIS—education is the answer to ignorance. Yes, I know education is hard. Yes, I am aware there are very steep learning curves. I have experienced many of them myself and have helped many clients through them. However, as Ben Franklin quipped, "The only thing more expensive than education is ignorance." In this case, the expense comes from lost opportunities in not knowing what the Preventing Stupid Method can teach you.

Building your BIS is a wholly subjective enterprise. It depends on your vision, your goals, your abilities, and your weaknesses. That is why, when working with clients, my first task is working on the system within them. Typically, this starts having positive effects on the overall business. Again, this is because continued, sustained success in business is dependent on the personal development of the owner. I know that the words "personal development" can offend many practical-minded business owners, as they see the idea as nebulous nonsense. Their skepticism makes sense unless we tailor their development exactly to the needs of their business, which is precisely what the Preventing Stupid Method allows us to do.

Beyond the owner, in building your BIS there are a litany of best practices to apply to a business. The question remains, what is the right way for your particular business? Again, this is a function of practicality, legality, and morality. As a learning tool, I will introduce you to fictional but compellingly realistic examples of the ways people run their businesses without regard to putting a BIS in place. The examples will make you cringe, as you will undoubtedly recognize your own vulnerabilities and mistakes in these stories. You will also see some of your successes. Before we get to those examples, I am going to give you some encouragement to understand why you need to build a solid BIS for your operation.

CHAPTER SUMMARY

✔ In creating a Business Immune System, it is often important to begin by first tackling problems that stem from the business owner.

✔ Using the Business Problem Severity Scale, the business can analyze what problems to address next.

Why You Can Build Your Business Immune System —How and Why You Can Prevent Stupid

———

WHEN I BROACH THE SUBJECT OF BUILDING A BIS, MORE OFTEN than not, I feel a wave of resistance emanating from the client. The point of this chapter is to prove that building a BIS is doable. At some point in your business career, you will decide to seek some professional assistance. Overcoming the learning curve requires identification and prioritization using the three questions we have worked with in earlier chapters. Then you must determine the right way for your business to work. Sometimes you can simply use a best-practices list from the internet. Other times require a custom answer. This process sets in motion a process of discovery about yourself and your business that will increase your learning curve, resulting in a much more confident owner and a much more profitable business.

Some people protest that they do not know where to begin. Others raise the objection that they do not know their business well enough to consider foreseeing the challenges ahead of them. In fact, these feelings are quite natural, and I acknowledge them as valid concerns. I have lived through it personally when building my firm and each time I help my clients build theirs.

The fear of not knowing what the future can bring paralyzes many business owners. They stay up at night tossing and turning about how things could go wrong. Fear of the unknown can eclipse their ability to move the business forward. Knowing the right questions to ask is the key to opening the door to these unknown problems. I have encouraged many business owners through this process. In doing so, I always return to the same three points, which I have sprinkled throughout this book:

- there is nothing new under the sun;
- piñata theory; and
- the tortoise and the hare.

These three points work in conjunction with one another in the following way:

There is no undiscovered territory; someone has done it all before. You just have to pick up your stick and start swinging at your goal—in this case, the piñata. Soon you will hit the piñata hard enough and get the candy. Remember that the methodical and steady hitter is the one that gets the candy. You do not have to be the most talented; rather, just keep your head and do not be stupid.

So, that is my standard pep talk in a paragraph. Now I will spend the rest of the chapter explaining it.

That there is nothing new under the sun should offer the initial dose of confidence to the business owner who thinks that the job ahead of him is an undiscovered country. In fact, it is exactly the opposite. People have been selling goods and services for thousands of years. The products and services may have changed, but there is nothing new in business. You are wise to study similar businesses so that you can maximize your return on your efforts by avoiding the mistakes people have made before you. These can be simple things like insuring your key manager, so that if he or she accidentally dies, you have a war chest fund to find a replacement; or preparing checklists for safety procedures for routine work, so that you do not end up in workers' compensation court.

This point applies to all businesses, whether the shop is Microsoft or a corner grocery. What this means for you is that you do not have to reinvent the wheel. There are best practices that apply to every business. Using an existent best-practices list saves time, as you can put them to work right away. For instance, you should have a plan together for who will run your business if you unexpectedly pass on, so that your family can continue to reap the rewards of your efforts. In the alternative, you should run your business in a way that makes it easily marketable, so that you or your family can sell it. The bottom line is, again, there is nothing new under the sun, and with a little pluck, you can build a successful business.

I have a client who, on a whim, decided to start a retail clothing boutique. She and her husband had a successful contracting business, but she wanted to do something more for herself. Really, what she wanted was to "be able to sell cute clothes at affordable prices to the moms that like to wear blue jeans and Converse." This idea was completely unexpected and had a wide stretch of new questions and challenges ahead of it. However, she knew they had built a business before and that, using what they had learned along the way in the first business, they could do it again, this time with a different product.

My firm started working with her early in the business, and we helped her focus on the priorities in building her business. We did this by helping her understand the seven working parts of the business. With those priorities set, which, by design, incorporated the three questions, the business took off at a rapid pace. She did not spend her time fixing problems, but instead used it constructively, so that the sales of the business increased at a blistering pace of 20 percent per month (that's right, per month) for the first year, or a total of 240 percent for the first year.

There were definitely brief moments of teeth gnashing and white-knuckle fear, but these all resolved into a confidence based on understanding the principle that there is nothing new under the sun. Every week she faced new challenges and issues. For instance, some providers refused to sell her their products unless she signed a contract promising that the goods would not sell at less than a 100 percent markup. She also had to deal with things like workers' compensation insurance and other employee issues. However, with the confidence she had that they had done this before, mastering the necessary tasks and skills allowed her to downgrade potential problems so they became hassles—easily corrected—and they did not develop into serious problems.

All these steps require action and effort on your part, and, in many instances, professional help from lawyers, accountants, and so forth. You have to take steps to prepare, identify, and implement these actions. It is incumbent on you to do this proactively. You are the leader. You must step out and make these things happen if you want to achieve peak performance, and thus peak income for your business. Remember, there is nothing new under the sun, and that gives you the advantage of being able to research how the others succeeded before you.

The next principle I call the piñata theory. This is the idea that Ralph Waldo Emerson expressed when he said, "Once you make a decision, the universe conspires to make it happen." While I am not on board with Emerson's characterization of this being the effect of an impersonal force, I am completely on board with the notion that once you commit to a good cause, the opportunities will jump out at you. Put a more biblical way, "The Lord helps those that help themselves." This is not to say that there will not be difficulties, obstacles, and failures. However, more often than not, the assistance that springs forth from unexpected sources will astound you. I have seen this repeatedly in both my business and in my clients' businesses as well.

When I am advising clients, I discuss the need just to get moving in terms of the piñata theory: you must pick up the stick and keep swinging if you want to get the candy! Clients can relate to that, because everyone likes party games and candy, right? Getting started is imperative; but unfortunately, with the piñata theory, you have a blindfold on, so you are swinging in the dark at a moving target. It is a bit tricky. In fact, your swings are random, and you are just lucky if you hit it.

My team knows that this is what I do, too. One of my clients had a problem with retention of its key employees. This complicated human resource problem was costing the business a good deal of money every year. We could not easily identify the issue or issues causing the problem. I actually went out, bought a piñata, and gave it a nice faux-Spanish name: Retention. I stuffed it with candy, and now it sits in my client's office so that every day it serves as a reminder that we are working on this issue. We have not solved it yet, but because we keep focused on it and continue taking swings at the problem, I anticipate we will crack the piñata open soon.

I am an unabashed advocate of the belief that good things happen once you pick up your stick and go after it. You begin to see things you need to do to move on to new levels of success, and the opportunities naturally fall in your lap. Imagine getting to play piñata without the blindfold, allowing you to get a peek at the problem. The three questions help you play at that level, and if you are lucky, you will receive the good fortune that comes to those who constantly keep trying, proving the old adage, "The harder I work, the luckier I get."

I have already referred to the tortoise and the hare, or my alternative version of rhythm and bass. The point I seek to make through this part of my lecture is that it is the slow, patient, and steady ones that win in the end. They are the ones who methodically think about what service or goods they can provide better than anyone else can. They may not do it with a bunch of flash and dash, but they do turn out huge profits. When these businesses prepare a solid BIS, they tend to skyrocket. This is because problems no longer distract the already disciplined owner or manager, who can instead focus on opportunities.

This principle should provide you even more comfort and calm because it takes the huge burden of being smart, brilliant, and exceptional off your shoulders. You do not have to be a rock star to run or build a business that is going to put tons of money in your pocket. That burden is not yours; in fact, if that is your goal, you will likely miss the important rhythm and bass that could have been the foundation of your success. You do not have to be Mick Jagger; if you'll be Charlie Watts (the Rolling Stones' drummer), you will fare better in the long run. This is not because you are not capable of rock-star status, because in fact, you've spent your life becoming a virtuoso at your trade, honing your skills to the level where you feel ready to run your own shop.

I have several clients who are low-key, easygoing people. Until you have spent time with them, you would never guess that they are successful business owners. This is because they keep their lives in balance and do not go overboard trying to be the hare in their line of work. They work slowly and steadily and do not make mistakes. This is in stark contrast to those we call "all hat, no cattle"—they are the businesspeople who spend their time talking about how successful they are. Chances are they are the hares of the race.

We address these three points in our dealings with clients as if they are on a repeat loop. I have found that most businesses, no matter how small, can benefit using these three principles, and go on to build a healthy BIS. The next step requires methodical movements and a little sound advice, and finally, the process becomes second nature. Experienced business owners know that running a company is a constant learning curve. I have a friend who says this better than anyone I know: "New level, new devil." What she means is that businesses are constantly in a state of growth, or else they start to atrophy. However, once your confidence increases, the growth becomes second nature and your business skills seem to multiply. This phenomenon is why the rich get richer. I presume that if you have made it this far in this book, you want to join that rank. The rest of this book will teach you, through abstract and then concrete examples, how you can improve your BIS.

CHAPTER SUMMARY

✔ You can create a successful BIS, because businesses have been doing the same, in some form, for years without crumbling.

✔ The piñata theory posits that a business owner must swing and miss a few times to achieve a goal. Creating a BIS is a swing that will eventually hit the piñata to release the candy.

✔ Steady and intentional planning is the key to success.

9

When to Start Preventing Stupid

I EXPECT THAT TO MANY PEOPLE WHO READ THIS BOOK, THE act of preventing stupid could seem very overwhelming. In fact, the opposite is true. Not preventing stupid is one of the key reasons the vast majority of small businesses fail and why many large businesses stumble. Thus, the truth is, the Preventing Stupid Method provides a way out. It provides hope that the risks of running a business are much more easily managed than typically thought. It outlines an efficient path to managing the pitfalls that absolutely and undoubtedly lie ahead of you when running a business. Remember, there is nothing new under the sun.

So, the question becomes when and how to start. The answer to the "when" question is easy—now! As to how, fortunately or unfortunately, I am a lawyer, and my default answer, as with every other question posed to a lawyer, is, "It depends." Seriously, in this case it really does. However, some common denominators provide guidelines of how to prevent stupid in your business. The two most important are the size of your revenue and the maturity of your business.

The denominator of the revenue stream is also one that Mike

Michalowicz addressed in his book *Profit First*, which is required reading for all my firm's custom legal department (CLD) clients.[1] Michalowicz's contribution is in simplifying and optimizing financial metrics. In *Profit First*, he relates the story about when he suggested to Michael Gerber—author of *The E-Myth* and perhaps the most astute small-business advisor in the world—that *The E-Myth* contained an inherent shortcoming, because it did not differentiate between the sizes of the businesses. This is a very relevant point in implementing the Preventing Stupid Method.

Gerber's genius is that he showed small businesses how to both simplify and optimize their production through systematization. Not incidentally, *The E-Myth* is also on the required-reading list for our clients. In *The E-Myth*, Gerber astutely outlines the different roles that a business owner must play in running a business. He divides the roles into the technician, the manager, and the entrepreneur. He points out that it is typically technicians (by which he means people skilled in a particular trade) who start businesses after having had their fill of working for "the man." I agree with him on this point, and additionally that they are nearly always unprepared for the roles they have now assumed as a manager and an entrepreneur.

Gerber's insight into this problem is that the new business owner should "work on" rather than "work in" the business. What this means is that business owners need to create systems that make their business work and that ensure consistency, so they are not juggling all the responsibilities of the business themselves. These are nothing more than habits, but habits enforced by written procedures detailing all the tasks of the business, both internally and externally. What Michalowicz pointed out is that at different stages of a business's growth and maturity, the role of implementing this systematization varies widely. The same is true for preventing stupid.

As an example of how the stage of a company's growth makes a difference, my firm generates much of what we call business issue leads from our internet advertising. These are small-business owners with a legal problem, such as with contracts, landlords, insurance companies, and so forth. We actively cultivate these clients both because they are one of our three core lines of business, but also because we want to help them grow and become CLD clients. These leads are very valuable to us, so we begin building the relationship right away. As the owner, I still handle a good number of the sales calls, but that will change as the firm grows.

From the inception of our firm, when I sign the case, my paralegal has been responsible for opening the files. I would hand the New File Intake form to her so she could open a new client file and get the work started. The problem with that procedure, now that my firm has grown to include a marketing department, is that the marketing people were not getting the message about the new file. To make matters worse, if we did not land the case on the first call, since the new lead information did not automatically go to marketing, they could not follow up on it to secure the client.

I knew this had to change, so I developed a new procedure. We considered a number of solutions, including various forms, slips, and email going around between my paralegal, our director of client services, and me. All these ideas just added another layer of complication to the system. Then the simple solution dawned on me: the director of client services can create the files and maintain my Prospective New Client forms.

Changing this habit solved two problems. First, it saved time and work for my already very busy paralegal. It also ensured that our marketing department got the necessary information to begin the job of cementing our relationship with the new client or prospect. In addition, they became involved in the relationship right from the start, which gave our clients a point of contact to rely on, and they appreciated it. We wrote up the process with input from everyone involved and implemented it, much to our relief. The result was a system that serves our clients, our prospects, and our firm better and does so in a way we can replicate.

With that example in mind, I want to bring us back to the question of how to implement the Preventing Stupid Method in your business. You will recall my earlier answer was, "It depends." The key factor that it depends on is the size of your business and the maturity of its systems. I use this example from my firm to illustrate both points that I weave together in this chapter. The procedure we implemented was a change in how we process new clients that came about because of the firm's growth. Prior to having a marketing department, things were just fine as they were.

However, as the firm grew, we needed to change how we applied Gerber's principles of systematization. Again, Gerber's point was to simplify and optimize the way a company turns out its product. Similarly, I designed the Preventing Stupid Method to simplify and optimize how a company protects itself from both internal and external threats. The protection requirements for a company depend on the size and construction of the company and its systems.

The application of Michalowicz's financial metrics, Gerber's systematization, and Preventing Stupid are all primarily dependent on the size of the business and the existence, or not, of systems. Please note that I use the word "primarily," because I have a common denominator of business in mind that makes up most of the companies that will be interested in implementing the Preventing Stupid Method. These businesses include startups and established businesses that still have an interest in growing or improving their operations.

I recognize that revenue, as an indicator of the size of a business, is inherently arbitrary. A service firm with minimal cost of goods is not an accurate comparison to a construction firm with substantial materials costs. An alternative method might be to differentiate companies by the number of employees, based on a rule of thumb that each employee should represent a specific revenue amount. I will outline several stages of a company's life span and show how to prioritize Preventing Stupid to achieve maximum effect. Aside from the arbitrariness of revenue as the denominator, there is also the fact that every company is inherently different. With that in mind, I have sought to weave some common threads together to illustrate how companies at four different stages might best build their Business Immune System.

Priorities for Startup to $250,000 in Revenue

When you are just starting out, you do not need a lot of protection, because you really do not have that much to lose. You need to plant the seeds of your BIS and focus on just a few areas. The following chart highlights the main areas where most startup businesses need to prioritize Preventing Stupid.

BUSINESS IMMUNE SYSTEM REPORT: PRIORITIES FOR COMPANIES JUST STARTING OUT		
	CATASTROPHE	IGNORANCE	INEPTITUDE
Management	Medium	High	Low
Personnel	Low	High	Low
Production	Low	High	Medium
Plant	Low	Low	Low
Metrics	Low	Medium	Low
Marketing	Medium	High	Medium
Sales	Medium	High	Medium

Figure 11: BISR for Startups

I do not mean that any of these areas are unimportant. Instead, I mean that the ones I have marked as high priority are the most common risk points for a startup business. Let me explain my reasons for these prioritizations and show you why my emphasis on this phase of a business focuses on eliminating ignorance through education.

Management: The reason catastrophe is just a medium priority in a startup business is because the business has little to lose. Yes, there are great hopes and dreams, but there are much more pressing things to be concerned about.

Foremost is the learning curve that the owner is undoubtedly experiencing. Unless the owner of this new venture has grown a business of the same kind before, there will be many kinks to work out and tricks of the trade to acquire. This is why education, the cure to ignorance, is critical at this phase. The pressing questions are, "What do we not know how to do?" and "How do we learn it?"

Ineptitude does not reach the same level of priority, because the owner (again, unless he or she is previously experienced) is just learning how to make his or her operation work. Ineptitude rises in priority once the company is up and running.

Personnel: Should a small startup have any employees, the priorities for risk management with them are similar to management. I rate concern about catastrophes low because it is unlikely that these employees are the personnel that will become key players in a $10 million–plus operation. If they are key players, then raise the priority. However, ignorance is critical. Just as the owner has a learning curve about all aspects of the business, all employees have a learning curve for their own tasks. In addition, with a startup, it is common for initial employees to wear more than one hat. The same two questions asked previously apply. Rooting out ineptitude matters, of course, but at this point, as a practical matter, addressing ignorance is just more relevant.

Production: As the company's operations begin, catastrophes tend to be small and recoverable. At this point, production is not so big that if necessary, creating it from scratch again is possible. Yes, it is important, but figuring out how to do it correctly is most critical, which is why the priority needs to be on asking the right questions to root out ignorance. The time to begin developing systems for dealing with mistakes, problems, and pitfalls is as soon as you discover them. At this point, documentation of production methods must begin for future systemization.

Plant: Again, presuming that this is a company headed for growth, I suggest a low priority for risk management for your physical plant across the board. The reason is that your shop, store, or office at this stage is likely more of a hotel than a home. You will outgrow it, so keep the investment of time and energy in it minimal. This does not mean to fail to insure it or educate yourself about what you need. Instead, focus more on you and your company's knowledge base rather than its location.

Metrics: Catastrophe gets a low rating because there is not much to measure yet in terms of things like cash flow and employee performance. Ignorance is more important because you need to be developing and learning about the metrics that will give you power in the management of your business. Ineptitude gets a low rating because the measurement systems are so basic that there is relatively little that can go wrong.

Marketing and Sales: I am grouping these together because they are the core focus of your company in this stage of growth. Your main job is to hustle, market, and sell. If you ever hope to achieve a higher level, you must learn how to ply your trade, sell your wares, and make a buck doing it. If you cannot figure this out, you are doomed to stay in the bush leagues.

Accordingly, catastrophe gets a medium rating, but this is not because you are not going to suffer failures. You *are* going to make mistakes in this process. The point of preventing catastrophe is not to make serious, company-killing ones. In contrast, ignorance gets a high rating because the best use of your energy is in learning from your mistakes. In fact, the lessons that you dedicate yourself to learning from your failures are the tricks of the trade that will propel your company to growth. These lessons will be some of the most valuable things your company will ever have. At this stage, you must rigorously scrutinize what works in your marketing and sales techniques and take those lessons to heart.

Ineptitude gets a medium rating because you need to begin to build your marketing plan and implement your sales techniques, such as the scripts that you follow when making calls. As these develop, it is important that you constantly update your sales and marketing techniques. Without this diligence, your system can easily falter (and your company with it).

Conclusion: For a small company set on growth, whether it is a brand-new startup or a company that has been in existence for a while and is now ready to grow, the key priorities are as follows:

- Management: Ignorance
- Personnel: Ignorance
- Production: Ignorance
- Marketing: Ignorance
- Sales: Ignorance

The simple reason for the commonality of ignorance is that, like a baby, this company needs to "learn things." It needs to learn how to walk before it can run. It needs to learn not only how to do the work of the company but also how to make money doing it. Education is the solution to ignorance. The toughest school is the school of hard knocks. So, the focus here is learning from others to minimize the number of critical mistakes, while also recognizing that failures are inevitable and that when they do happen, you will learn their valuable lessons.

Priorities for $250,000 to $1,000,000 in Revenue

Once your company has surpassed $250,000 in revenue, you have most likely mastered the art of selling and marketing your goods or services. Presuming a general rule of thumb that each employee should account for about $200,000 in revenue, which I acknowledge is a grossly inaccurate rule, then you are in a position to begin to delegate some of your work and management responsibilities. This changes your risk profile and thus your priorities in preventing stupid. The following chart maps out a recommended list of priorities based on companies in this range of revenue.

BUSINESS IMMUNE SYSTEM REPORT: PRIORITIES FOR COMPANIES WITH $250,000 TO $1,000,000 IN REVENUE			
	CATASTROPHE	IGNORANCE	INEPTITUDE
Management	High	High	Medium
Personnel	Medium	High	Medium
Production	Medium	High	Medium/High
Plant	Medium	Medium	Low
Metrics	Medium	High	Low
Marketing	Medium	High	Medium
Sales	Medium	High	Medium

Figure 12: BISR for Companies $250,000–$1,000,000

Management: At this point, the owner is still likely the CEO of the company. This company has something to lose, as does the owner's family, presuming they have decent profit margins or have a company they can sell. Protecting the business from the loss of the owner through insurance is critical, as is building up leaders in personnel.

Additionally, the owner is entering a completely new territory of business management. Rather than the owner occupying most of the positions on the organizational chart, other personnel are beginning to populate it. The owner is at a "new level, new devil," not only with the management of the new team members but also with the other systems of the business. This requires constant vigilance of the shortcomings and gaps in the owner's management skill set and a continuous dedication to self-education.

Ineptitude also becomes more relevant to keep an eye on as the owner hands off the work to the growing team.

Personnel: The team is starting to build at this point, so keep an eye on what Jim Collins called in his book *Good to Great* "getting the right people on the bus." At this point in your business growth, the employees become more vital to the growth trajectory and harder to replace. This warrants a medium level of scrutiny regarding losing them, particularly the ones with promise as future leaders.

In contrast, the team needs to learn how to do their jobs and do them well. Given the growth of the company, this means expanding their capabilities and educating them on the things they do not know. Therefore, understanding what your employees need to learn and then educating them remains a high priority. At this stage, it may mean plugging in fractional professionals (for instance, in accounting or marketing) to fill gaps in the team until the company can afford to bring these functions in-house.

At the higher end of the revenue range, the owner and the budding managers are starting to systematize the business as they work themselves up to higher levels of the organizational chart. Cementing the work habits of the employees that take their places also garners a higher level of priority than when the company was smaller.

Production: My reasoning for the priorities in production mirrors that for personnel. Now is the time to start building the systems that will allow the core team members to hand off work to the incoming team members. Catastrophe ranks at medium because you now have more to lose due to both the size of the operation and the complexity of it.

Overcoming ignorance by continuing to learn and refine your production is key. This stage is like being a teenager: you may think you know what you are doing, but reflecting as an adult you will wonder what in the world you were thinking. Incidentally, that feeling never ends, but at this stage, the knowledge gap remains mammoth. Education and refining production are super-high priorities.

Ineptitude gets a medium/high rating because of the growing importance of you and your team perfecting the systems that work for your business. Again, this is a critical time to work on your business, as identifying problems now is critical for both present and future production. One key reason for the split decision on priority is, as you reach the upper level of this revenue range, the priority drifts toward a high rating, which is where it lands in the next stage of growth.

Plant: Protecting your plant from catastrophe takes on a bit of a higher level of priority because you have more to lose. Generally, this is not your highest concern, because your business focus needs to be on gaining knowledge and experience. Do not ignore this concern; just keep your eye on the prize.

The same reasoning follows through with ignorance. Ultimately, with ineptitude it tapers down to a low priority in contrast to the other concerns.

Metrics: Through this phase of growth, you should be running your business on the metrics you gather. This includes financial, operations, marketing, and other data. You need to secure and protect this data because it is the critical construction material for your growth as the CEO. Still, this ranks as a medium priority (in contrast to learning what you still need).

As you build the company through this stage, you must be constantly watching both potential and present problems to develop metrics to steer around them. As my firm grew, I developed a metric we call Attorney Month. This is an aggregate measurement of the team production by our key revenue generators that really helps me measure performance. You will find and develop similar metrics as you prioritize educating yourself.

Ineptitude is not as high of a priority mainly because you have not fully built this system. You need to focus more on getting the act together rather than making sure it is perfect. That can wait for later. Dialing it in is important, but if you do not have the metrics set fully developed, that is where you need to focus first.

Marketing and Sales: The priorities for these two systems track each other again. The core reason is that the business is now the size that the owner is likely not the primary business generator and signer. This is particularly true at the upper end of the revenue range. Others must take on these jobs as the owner begins to run an increasingly complex organization.

Preventing catastrophes is a medium priority because the marketing and sales systems are starting to take hold, although developing and perfecting them continues to be important. Thus, the high priority here is education and development. As these systems grow, take the necessary steps to ensure they are duplicable. The checklist and procedures need building, which is why ineptitude gets a medium rather than a low priority.

Conclusion: For a still-growing company ramping up to over a million in revenue, the key priorities are as follows:

- Management: Catastrophe and Ignorance
- Personnel: Ignorance
- Production: Ignorance
- Metrics: Ignorance
- Marketing: Ignorance
- Sales: Ignorance

The emphasis is still clearly on learning how to make the company run smoothly. The metaphor of a teenager is apt because while in many ways the company is starting to look like a mature organization, it still lacks experience and judgment. This is why focusing on what the team does not know and improving their skill sets make up the highest priorities.

Priorities for $1,000,000 to $10,000,000 in Revenue

Presuming you have started to build your systems and have handed key job functions to team members, by necessity your priorities will change. This is a company with much to lose. Very few small businesses reach this size. This phase is when real maturing needs to happen to turn a going concern into a life-changing legacy. Here is the chart of the priorities for accomplishing that:

BUSINESS IMMUNE SYSTEM REPORT: PRIORITIES FOR COMPANIES WITH $1,000,000 TO $10,000,000 IN REVENUE			
	CATASTROPHE	**IGNORANCE**	**INEPTITUDE**
Management	High	High	High
Personnel	High	Medium	Medium
Production	Medium	Medium	High
Plant	Medium	Low	Low
Metrics	Medium	High	High
Marketing	Medium	High	Medium
Sales	Medium	High	High

Figure 13: BISR for Companies $1,000,000–$10,000,000

Management: At this point, you have built a business that has something to lose. Here you need to concern yourself with what happens to you, the owner. Again, unless the owner has previously run a sizable business, ignorance remains of critical importance. There is a lot of "undiscovered country" between $1 million and $10 million. The learning curve may not be as steep as that of a newly spun entrepreneur, but it is still there. Ineptitude starts to become more critical as well. The owner now must have the valuable skills needed to make the business work.

Personnel: Through this phase of growth, the key members of the team become increasingly vital and hard to replace. This is where serious questions need asking in case a catastrophe strikes one of them. Additionally, the workers need consideration, because the team is bigger and they play a critical role. You will need to pay attention to your key manager's education about the business. However, as the workers' roles become more specialized, they become easier to manage than when the key team members wore many hats. Ineptitude tracks a similar reasoning.

Production: Catastrophes are now a medium priority because of the size of the operation. The knowledge base of the company is higher now that you have resolved the kinks from the earlier growth. This knowledge keeps ignorance from being a high priority, even though it still warrants medium priority. Ineptitude, however, is more critical, because to push the company to the next level, the team must remain diligent. You will need to improve development of the systems that strengthen the techniques and practices that brought the company to this point.

Plant: This is the lowest concern of all the systems. The plant needs protection, which mainly means insurance. However, because it is already up and running, ignorance and ineptitude are low priorities.

Metrics: A business of this size is really starting to rely on the metrics to make management decisions. While catastrophe rates at medium priority, both ignorance and ineptitude are high priorities. This is because there are still metrics to develop and implement to drive top performance and keep track of them as they take hold. The metrics take on a completely new level of sophistication through this phase of growth and demand significant attention.

Marketing and Sales: Again, these two track each other, except for sales getting a higher priority in ineptitude. Both systems still need ongoing development and improvement. The emphasis on sales ineptitude is to ensure that your sales team is employing the lessons learned along the way to close the deals so that your revenue does not taper off.

Conclusion: For a company approaching maturity, the key priorities are as follows:

- Management: Catastrophe and Ignorance
- Personnel: Catastrophe
- Production: Ineptitude
- Metrics: Ignorance
- Marketing: Ignorance
- Sales: Ignorance and Ineptitude

This stage of growth is like young adulthood. This is the time to perfect the skill sets and to integrate and cement the lessons learned along the way into the operations. In addition, management has so many things to concern themselves with that the data has to be readily available and reliable. Marketing and sales still need improvement to push the revenue growth to the next level.

Priorities for More Than $10,000,000 in Revenue

This is a mature company. The owner should be working on the business rather that in it, or even enjoying the fruits of his or her labor with more leisure time. The senior management team has gelled. Protecting the company from catastrophes to this group and the owner is critical. Their hard work and perseverance created a business that runs well, but making sure the operations do not fall apart due to a lack of care becomes the other key focus. The priorities map out as follows:

**BUSINESS IMMUNE SYSTEM REPORT: PRIORITIES FOR
COMPANIES WITH MORE THAN $10,000,000 IN REVENUE**

	CATASTROPHE	IGNORANCE	INEPTITUDE
Management	High	Low	Medium
Personnel	High	Low	Medium
Production	Low	Low	High
Plant	Low	Low	Low
Metrics	Low	Low	High
Marketing	Low	Low	Medium
Sales	Low	Low	High

Figure 14: BISR for Companies More Than $10,000,000

Management: At this point, the owner may or may not still be at the helm, but protecting the leadership from catastrophe is critical to the long-term viability of the company. Getting a succession plan in place is crucial, as is having a bench of capable lieutenants. Ignorance becomes less of a concern because the owner and anyone he or she has selected as a replacement should have the requisite knowledge to run the business. Ineptitude, however, should get a medium level of priority, because this is the stage when owners can start to rest on their laurels and get sloppy in management.

Personnel: The priorities of personnel and the reasons for them mirror those of management. The team needs protection and the bench needs building. Presumably, the team knows what it is doing, but they still need watching to ensure that the work does not become slipshod.

Production: The production is now substantial, and the protections against catastrophe built in long ago. For similar reasons, ignorance is a low priority. This is because the team should know how to do the work of the business. There is still a need to educate the new members. In contrast, ineptitude becomes a high priority because you must make sure the team does the work it knows how to do.

Plant: The plant should be up and running. As such, it is a low priority.

Metrics: The measurements should all be in place and running smoothly at this stage of growth; however, whether they are receiving attention is another issue. A business this size can hide many pathologies. Making sure the team is not sleepwalking the business to a disaster is why ineptitude is at a high priority.

Marketing: The likelihood of a marketing disaster is low and the priority reflects this. Similarly, by now the company should know how to reach its customers and prospects. Making sure that marketing brings leads to sales is why ineptitude remains at a medium priority.

Sales: Like marketing, the sales team should not be susceptible to catastrophes and should know how to close a deal. Whether they remain hungry enough to do so is the concern. A team resting on its laurels can severely hurt a business.

Conclusion: For a mature company, the priorities are considerably different from those of a growing company. The priorities shift to be more concerned about protecting the core management team and keeping ineptitude from hampering performance. They are as follows:

- Management: Catastrophe
- Personnel: Catastrophe

- Production: Ineptitude
- Metrics: Ineptitude
- Sales: Ineptitude

Thinking about the transition to the next generation running the company is critical. Likewise, making sure the systems are running effectively, efficiently, and consistently becomes a high priority.

As with all of Preventing Stupid, how and where to start is an art, not a science. The two interrelated factors of size and maturity have a significant impact on how to work on building your Business Immune System. They are interrelated because it is likely that if your business has reached a certain size, it has grown in the maturity of its systems and operations as well. This is not always the case, but it is a common denominator, which necessarily means there will be outliers to the rule.

The general drift is that priorities shift from overcoming ignorance to preventing catastrophe and warding off ineptitude. This is part of the natural growth of a business from infancy to maturity. This is why children need to learn but do not need large amounts of life insurance. Somewhere in this natural progression of business, the art of preventing stupid attaches to help you improve and protect your business.

CHAPTER SUMMARY

✔ The application of the Preventing Stupid Method is primarily dependent on the size of the business and the existence, or not, of systems.

✓ For a small company set on growth, the focus is to learn from others to minimize the number of critical mistakes, while also recognizing that failures are inevitable and can offer valuable lessons.

✓ For a still-growing company ramping up to over a million in revenue, the focus is to learn how to make the company run smoothly and improve skill sets.

✓ For a company approaching maturity, the focus is to perfect the skill sets and integrate and cement the lessons learned along the way.

✓ For a mature company, the focus is to make sure systems are running effectively, efficiently, and consistently and to think about the transition to the next generation running the company.

✓ As companies grow, priorities shift from overcoming ignorance to preventing catastrophe and warding off ineptitude.

Catastrophes in General

IF YOU ARE READY FOR THEM, CATASTROPHES CAN BE EXHILA-rating and rewarding. If you are not, they can be nothing less than devastating. Not preparing for foreseeable catastrophes can cost you your entire business—or at the very least, it can set you back financially and hamper your long-term plans. Catastrophes are going to happen; that is a given. The thing to focus on is preventing them from adversely affecting your business, by either warding them off altogether or being prepared to deal with them. This chapter is a brief examination of the different types of catastrophes you may encounter while running your business.

The first question you need to address is, "What types of catastrophes are most likely to strike my business?" For example, high on my list are ice storms in the winter, because I've dealt with them where I live, and when they happen, the power can go out for days—so a good generator and a stock of gasoline are necessary. Hurricanes, however, are not high on my list.

Most catastrophes do not hit you as full-force natural disasters; in fact, in the law business, we call these "acts of God." Instead, most catastrophes happen as acts of humanity, and these can come from anywhere.

A natural disaster is actually more predictable and easier to manage. A tornado, flood, or hurricane can wipe your business off the face of the earth, but that is why you have insurance. Do not doubt the creativity of the insurance companies in developing their products! However, the human element of business catastrophes is a trickier matter.

The curious thing about the act-of-humanity type of catastrophes is that they come from two sources: you and other people. The latter sort we can label as "human," because they relate to disasters brought on by the actions or omissions of other people associated with your business. These individuals can be employees, vendors, or customers, or others. Their negligent accidents, malicious acts, or careless deeds can ruin your business as quickly as a bowie knife ruins a tire. These human catastrophes can be every bit as devastating as a tornado or a fire burning your shop to the ground. Frankly, they are a lot more common.

Next are the catastrophes you bring on yourself. I label these as internal catastrophes. These are a little tricky to understand and in some ways bleed over into ignorance and ineptitude categories. That said, once you recognize that your business is a reflection of the thoughts and dreams in your own mind, it starts to make more sense. More specifically, you will confine your business by how you see its possibilities. It will also run only as well as you run it.

As an example of the power of a vision—Henry Ford did not make the first car, but he envisioned that he was going to make the Model T available and affordable for average, everyday Americans. Ford Motor Company fulfilled that vision. Mark Zuckerberg saw Facebook turning into a massive social media enterprise with all sorts of revenue opportunities from advertising. Facebook fulfilled this vision as well.

I am using billionaires (adjusted to today's dollars, in Ford's case) as examples not because you are likely to become a billionaire if you can envision a business, but because we all probably know who they are. Their examples demonstrate the power of the idea behind a business. Also, and more importantly, they avoided internal catastrophes while building their businesses. The point is, they were able to dream and see it through—and not stand in their own way.

Being able to recognize what you are doing to stifle your business's growth can be a difficult skill to learn. I am sure you have heard the adage that we are all our own worst enemies. This holds true in business as well. It leads to subtle, insidious, and sometimes hard-to-detect psychological and emotional barriers that cause business owners to get in their own way.

In small businesses, most frequently the problem lies in getting the owner to let go of his or her stranglehold over one or more of the seven working parts of the business. Business owners can be very controlling and can tend to micromanage. This micromanagement can put a choke hold on any aspect of the business, and this will prevent growth in those systems of their business. Sometimes the problem is rooted in the very practical issue of delegating tasks, such as sales or the day-to-day production functions of the business.

This type of internal catastrophe is problematic for business owners—it's when they just cannot let go of their precious business. They built it. It is their baby, and no one can do it as they can. The owners tell themselves that their customers will never settle for doing business with anyone less than them. This attitude reminds me of some law firms in my market who fixate on their legacy, or the idea that they have been in business since time immemorial. As if anyone cares! I bought into that thinking when I was a greenhorn lawyer, but I soon got over it when I realized my clients just wanted a job done and I was effectively a plumber pushing paper.

Beyond the human and internal catastrophes, the owner's goals also carve out another distinction, and that is the difference between objective and subjective catastrophes. It is obvious that everybody has different goals, dreams, and objectives. Sometimes a catastrophe, like beauty, is in the eye of the beholder. If you have a dream of growing your business so junior can go to private school, but you will not hire that new employee you need to up your revenue to that level, well, that is a latent subjective catastrophe. If you are content to let opportunities pass you by and not try to grow your business, then that is just fine. Some things are a catastrophe to one business owner that are not to another. As they say, that is why they make both chocolate and vanilla ice cream.

The distinctions I just illustrated create six different categories of catastrophes. First, you have the natural, human, and internal across the top row. If you apply the objective and subjective as I did here along the left column, you end up with a table that looks like this:

	NATURAL	HUMAN	INTERNAL
Objective			
Subjective			

Figure 15: Categories of Catastrophes

Recognizing these six distinctions enables you to put a finer point on how to look at the catastrophes that might affect your business. Using this table will help you organize and narrow down catastrophes to six questions starting with,

1. What objective natural catastrophes could strike my business?

and ending with,

6. What subjective internal catastrophes could strike my business?

We use these six questions to help our clients get a handle on what potential disasters they should prepare for. It is also an extremely useful tool to determine whether there are any real priorities among the list. Asking yourself these specific questions will help you to clearly and accurately think through and prepare for any disasters coming at you in the future. This way of thinking turns an overwhelming task into a manageable job.

In essence, it is applying the "elephant principle." How do you eat an elephant? One bite at a time. Breaking your business down into bite-sized pieces lets you do just that. This first step of the deconstruction of the types of catastrophes further allows you to start asking questions about how they might affect your business. This includes the likelihood of their occurrence and the other attributes of problems that I addressed in chapter 2.

As a generic exercise in this analysis, the following is a partial list of possible catastrophes that can affect you and your business.

The first is you. What if you fall ill and die? What is your family going to do? What about your key man or woman, the one you entrusted to manage the business in your stead? What if he or she dies, or even worse, your main competitor hires him or her away, and that awesome skill set you fostered in him or her is now a tool for someone else's use?

What if your largest customer changes its business model and stops using your product or service, or your main supplier no longer makes the part or material that you need? Did you notice that I just listed examples of how catastrophes might strike the seven working parts of your business?

The "nothing new under the sun" principle I spoke of earlier is applicable right here and is again great news. Human nature is what it is, and in the macro sense, it is predictable. Despite the long list of possible catastrophes, a number of them are so common that every business owner should be ready for them. There are even more catastrophes about which the business owner whose business has grown to the level of having employees will need to be concerned. That said, there are best practices to deal with all of them and getting those in place is what responsible business owners do. Again, this is not about being smart. None of this is rocket science. It is about recognizing potential issues, taking charge, and doing your job.

Once you put your information into the categories of the BISR, it becomes a lot easier to customize and prepare a plan to prevent the catastrophes from causing you harm. This boils the questions down into categories such as

- What sort of disasters could strike me that could screw up the business?
- What could go wrong with my employees that could make a mess of things?
- What problems with my vendors could make a total disaster for our cash flow?

I work hard not to focus too much on the fear of what these potential catastrophes can do to a business. At the end of the day, I am a realist and always go back to what Calvin Coolidge said: "If you see ten troubles coming down the road, you can be sure that nine will run into the ditch before they reach you." This point still holds true. The point of management is planning for the one that does reach you, and that, my friends, is your job and your duty.

Turning once again to the presidents for a little insight, Dwight Eisenhower said, "Plans are nothing, planning is everything." Eisenhower knew that all hell was going to break loose the second the troops hit the beaches of Normandy, yet they planned extensively. That was because somewhere, sometime in the heat battle, that planning was going to be indispensable in saving a life or winning a skirmish. It is all you *can* do, because we cannot predict the future. However, we can use forethought to make some educated guesses at it.

This chapter gave me a chance to discuss catastrophes in general and in the abstract. While that is useful, a more concrete, if fictional, example of how to use the BISR to prepare a business for the inevitable catastrophes follows in chapter 10. In that chapter I am going to walk you through an analysis of a fictional company as an exercise in how to size up and put together a responsible and reasonable catastrophe-prevention plan.

CHAPTER SUMMARY

✔ Survey what catastrophes are most likely to strike your business and prepare for those first.

✔ Categorize catastrophes in six ways using two label types: objective versus subjective and then natural, human, or internal.

✔ By categorizing potential catastrophes, a business owner can create a more manageable list of steps needed to prevent and prepare for them.

Red's Plumbing:
A Case Study in Catastrophes

———

IN THIS CHAPTER, WE EXAMINE A SMALL BUSINESS AND DIS-
cuss some of the things that the owner can do to help prepare the
business in the event of various catastrophes. The plan we will follow
is to evaluate potential catastrophes using a pared-down version of the
BISR. Our fictional company, which we will call Red's Plumbing, has
the following attributes:

- James is the red-haired, hot-tempered owner affectionately
  known to his friends as Red. He is thirty-nine years old.
- He worked for a medium-sized plumbing company from when
  he was just a couple years out of high school until he became
  fed up with his boss, the owner, for a litany of reasons—some
  good, some bad.
- Red started his company three years ago with just a truck and
  a few tools.
- He and his wife, Stephanie, have three kids at home between
  five and thirteen.
- Red's Plumbing is a sole proprietorship.

- The company grossed $100,000 its first year in business and ran a 20 percent profit margin.

- The margins have stayed the same into the third year, where the company should gross $250,000.

- Red now has one skilled journeyman plumber working for him—a friend from his old job whom he lured away from their prior mutual employer—and two apprentice plumbers.

- Red is still in the trenches either doing jobs with his team or solo jobs, and he also bids a few construction jobs when he gets time to do so.

- Stephanie helps take the orders for the shop. They converted the shop from the existing two-car garage on the back of their small acreage.

- Stephanie also does payroll and handwrites the checks.

- Stephanie only sporadically processes the invoices for services performed because she has a lot on her plate with raising the kids. Sometimes two weeks or more pass before Stephanie can send out the invoices for work completed.

- They use a desktop computer with no cloud backup for all billing and all other record keeping.

- There are no written policies, procedures, or systems about how to run the office or how to do the plumbing work. Also, no employee handbook exists.

- Red has not figured out whether he wants to work primarily on responsive service calls or on construction jobs.

- Red's service market is a medium-sized city of 250,000 people, with moderate growth, and the economy is stable.

- Red's Plumbing has a rudimentary website that a friend of theirs set up a year ago. It has no search engine optimization and no Google AdWords.

- They rely mostly on word of mouth for their business, including jobs that Red's friends in construction trades get for him.

- Nobody is monitoring Amy's List or similar sites; however, the reviews and recommendations listed for Red's Plumbing are generally positive.

- Red's purchases their insurance from an independent agent who is the husband of one of Stephanie's best childhood friends. They have a $1 million commercial general liability policy, appropriate workers' compensation coverage, and a $250,000 term life insurance policy on Red that has eighteen years left on it.

- Both Red and Stephanie want the kids to go to college. It seems like the best way for them to have a good life, but they cannot really state reasons why. It just seems like the right thing to do, and that's what business owners' kids are supposed to do.

- They have not planned how large they want the company to grow because they have not planned their optimal income or retirement needs.

Red's is a common small-business story, although the business can be a gold mine if they can organize and plan their actions. First, Red and Stephanie need to plan for the catastrophes that could put an end to their dreams. Again, most likely only one out of ten will hit them, but being prepared for that one can mean the difference between saving and losing their company and their livelihood.

With these facts laid out, I will use the Catastrophe column of the BISR to illustrate the key threats for their business. I graded Red's below; and remember, these grades are not a reflection on Red or Stephanie—rather, they are an assessment of the strength of the company's BIS. For instance, I gave Red's a C in management because of the lack of protection and because Red is still acting like a technician rather than a business owner. However, Red is only thirty-nine, so the likelihood of him dying anytime soon is a lot smaller than if he were sixty-nine. In that instance, I would have given Red's an F.

Following the BISR, I explain the reason for the given grades. When my team and I do a BISR for our clients, we explain the grades in writing and then discuss them in person. Because this book does not afford me that opportunity, I will illustrate my reasoning through anecdotes to help convey why catastrophes are a big threat to Red's business.

In analyzing Red's Plumbing, and as the basis for making the recommendations that follow, I would give the following grades for the Catastrophe column of the BISR:

	1: CATASTROPHE
1: Management	C
2: Personnel	C
3: Production	B
4: Plant	B
5: Metrics	C
6: Marketing	F
7: Sales	F

Figure 16: Catastrophe Only: Red's Plumbing BISR

1:1 Catastrophe in Management

We begin with Red. As the business owner, if he should die unexpectedly, the entire business will suffer or possibly cease to exist. The life insurance is not nearly enough. At this point, he should have at least $1 million to $2 million in coverage. In addition, he can change from being the sole proprietor of the business to being the entrepreneur of the company that owns the business. For a small investment and a little regular maintenance, he can form a limited liability company or corporation that protects all the personal assets he and his wife are building from an accident happening in the business. As the company grows, the tax advantages of electing to be a small-business corporation under the federal tax laws weigh in favor of a limited liability entity.

Because Red's work is still important to the business in generating money, his disability would be a major blow to the family's income. They should take a sound look at getting some disability coverage. The kids are a bit young to think about which one of them might want to take over, and their hopes of sending the kids to college will make it less likely that they will want to take over the company. Consequently, Red needs to gear his succession planning toward making the business a salable asset, either to one of the workers that might want to take it over or to an outside party. This way if something unforeseen were to happen to him, Stephanie has something to sell to support her family rather than just having to watch it evaporate.

2:1 Catastrophe in Personnel

There are two key employees in the company, Stephanie and the journeyman. Red would be in trouble if he lost either of them, but let's start with Stephanie, because she would be the greater loss on many levels. If Stephanie were in a fatal car accident, the shop would be in shambles. Not only did they just lose all the passwords she kept in her head but also the back-office work that made sure the money kept rolling in. It would be a huge problem if she died or if she was no longer able to work.

Since she is so important to the business, there is an "insurable interest" in her, so key person insurance would be in order. This sort of coverage pays out if Stephanie dies or if she cannot work due to a catastrophe. Red should also have some life insurance on her. With Stephanie gone, there would be a lot of added expense for the required domestic help for the kids. Obviously, losing his wife would take a huge personal toll on Red, but these steps would help with his business in a very difficult time.

A good relationship with the journeyman plumber makes it unlikely that he will leave the company, but it is always a possibility. While he and Red have been close friends for years, things happen. He could end up taking a job with a competitor or have a midlife crisis and decide he has always wanted to live in a ski town. If he dies, takes another job, or decides that the Rocky Mountains are calling, Red should have some key person insurance on him as well.

Then there are all the other employees. Red is trying to grow this business, and even losing an apprentice puts a dent in those plans. In order to sustain the growth Red wants for his business, he needs to have some feelers out and be ready to replace any losses in personnel. While in most places there are strict limitations on noncompetition agreements, as I mentioned earlier, nonsolicitation agreements are generally more enforceable. These agreements allow Red to protect his customer base. Although these agreements may not always be enforceable, often just the threat of them can keep employees from creating problems for the business owner.

Fortunately, Red's insurance broker did set up workers' compensation insurance, but the $1 million limit on his commercial coverage should be higher. It is a very common occurrence for a company's employee to get into an accident on company time. Medical costs or death claims can quickly mount up well beyond the $1 million limit. Given the heavy vehicles the crew is driving, the coverage is much too low.

3:1 Catastrophe in Production

Red and Stephanie want their company to grow, but right now, they have all the systems that make the business run in their heads. Sure, Red and the journeyman know how to go out and do the jobs. They know the trade and know how the business works. The journeyman knows because he and Red have worked side by side for years, and Red has taught him well. That one-on-one education is a luxury that not even his first batch of apprentices will get.

If Red and Stephanie want their business to grow, they are going to have to let go of some of their hands-on control, or their need to micromanage. This is the key to scalability, and it seems lost on Red and Stephanie. They need the assurances that their employees are not going to do subpar jobs that leave houses flooded, with weekend calls to repair the bad work and angry customers in the wake. The way to do this is through establishing written policies and procedures, which, when used together, make up the systems that let business owners like

Red and Stephanie sleep at night. Getting these in place really straddles preventing all three kinds of failure discussed in this book, but since we are examining catastrophe in this chapter, I will focus on that. Even at this stage of the business, their apprentices can go out unsupervised on easy side jobs for the company. Fortunately, Red provides his people with smart-looking uniforms from UniPlus. However, has he trained them how to treat a customer politely and with respect? Do they know how to write down their labor and materials correctly? Do they know how to get their billing information back to Stephanie and when to do so? As the company grows, the list of questions also grows. The way to prevent potential problems and know the answers to these questions is to prepare written policies and procedures. This saves the business owner a great deal of stress.

The policies are the company's internal rules and the procedures are how the company's employees are to go about doing their work. For instance, Red's policies might look like this:

- We expect all employees to be at the shop at 8:00 a.m. ready to work, dressed in their uniform with their shirt tucked in and a belt on.
- Weekend on-call assignments will be based on a rotating schedule, and all journeymen and apprentices with at least one year of on-the-job experience are on the rotation.
- All employees will treat our customers with the utmost respect and always remember that the customer is first.

These polices set the ground rules for the team and provide the basis for discipline if an employee cannot operate within the rules.

When you combine them with written procedures outlining how to complete the tasks properly, you end up with systems that relieve Red's stress level about how his employees are doing their jobs. Some examples of procedures might look like this:

- All employees will account for their time and materials on the carbon copy invoices stored in the bins by the back door on the north side of the shed. We expect each employee to make sure there are at least twenty-five of these in his or her vehicle when leaving the shop each morning to ensure adequate record keeping and billing.
- Each employee is to treat our customers with the utmost respect. When going to a job, even a weekend or after-hours emergency call, employees are to be in uniform, greet our customers with a friendly smile, and are to identify themselves by their name badge, saying, "Hi, I'm _____ with Red's Plumbing. We're here to help! Would you please show me where the problem is?"
- Complete all jobs strictly to code. Red's is not a "duct tape and bailing wire" outfit. You will see many shoddy jobs done by our competitors and DIY people. We are a by-the-code company, and we do all work accordingly. Every truck will have a codebook in it to ensure ready accessibility.

That last policy example straddles the line between a policy and procedure. It sets forth the rules but also provides a reference with the availability of the codebook. All of these items compiled become the company's policies and procedures manual, with some items outlining catastrophe prevention and some staving off ignorance and ineptitude. Because a standard operating procedures manual covers all three types of failure, we will revisit this subject in the upcoming chapters.

4:1 Catastrophe in the Physical Plant

There are also catastrophes that can strike the physical plant of the business. At Red's Plumbing, the main physical plant is the garage-turned-shop. Neither Red nor Stephanie checked to see whether they needed separate coverage on the shop, because they just assumed that their home or commercial general liability coverage would include shop coverage. Despite the fact that they put their shop together on a shoestring, it has now actually built some real value. A fire or other accident could cost more than $75,000, requiring replacement of the building and the equipment stored in it. A call to the insurance agent is definitely in order.

The nature of the business also means that a good deal of the physical plant is mobile. Red and his team are on the road all day fixing leaks and rooting out lines. Several of Red's trucks on the road are worth an average of $20,000 apiece. That is what they are worth currently; with all of the use attending to customers, they have very high mileage. To replace one truck new and fit it with all the necessary gear could easily run $50,000. Multiply that cost by the thirty-plus units Red's has on the road, and you understand the value of the mobile portion of Red's physical plant, and how much it would cost Red to replace it. Imagine what would happen if several of these high-mileage vehicles should break down at the same time. Again, time to make that call to the insurance agent.

5:1 Catastrophe in Metrics

By metrics, I mean the data that gives you the information to make good decisions for your business. You need it if you want to move forward successfully. The data compilations include, but certainly are not limited to, the financial information. It also extends to the other areas of the business, from the owner's time off, to marketing, to customer data.

For instance, one year I ran an analysis of my solo practice's cases from the prior year. I opened 130 files, and of these, only 20 represented new client business. Sounds pretty good, right? Those numbers show lots of repeat word-of-mouth business. That is actually fantastic for an outfit seeking to stay stable. However, it is an outright catastrophe for a growing business. Fortunately, those numbers were from before I decided to grow the firm, and with that information in hand, I was able to make sound decisions about marketing.

Meanwhile, back at Red's, Stephanie has the most control over the company's metrics. Fortunately, compiling this information is easy thanks to easy-to-use accounting programs. Unfortunately, Stephanie does not have a solid backup for the data that she does have. This is incredibly easy to accomplish with a call to an information-technology company. They can set up an external hard drive backup if you cannot. Given that the building can suffer damage, it is a good idea to sign up with an online backup company like Carbonite, IDrive, or Mozy. It is unlikely the destruction of both your shop and the abandoned salt mine where the backup company keeps their servers will occur at the same time. If it does, it is probably due to a thermonuclear war, so you will not care anyway.

Losing what little data Stephanie has would be an awful and costly mess. A sound data-preservation strategy, such as the online backup, is the key to preventing this type of catastrophe. Again, I am focusing solely on the catastrophes that can occur with your metrics, but Red's business is keeping only the most rudimentary metrics of what they need. We will get to those issues when we get to ignorance and ineptitude. For now, suffice it to say that there is some real stupid coming the way of Red's Plumbing if they fail to prevent this catastrophe.

6:1 Catastrophe in Marketing

Red's marketing is a catastrophe in the making—and likely not in the ways that are readily apparent. Getting new business in the house is the key to growing the company and achieving Red and Stephanie's dreams. They have not thought very much about how to accomplish this because they spend their time in the hustle and bustle of raising kids and running their business. Likewise, they have not given much thought to how to reach out to potential customers or what their desired customer base looks like. There is plenty to say about this situation in the Ignorance column, but since we are discussing catastrophes, let's deal with it all as a bundle.

The potential long-range catastrophes come from the weakness of this system as a whole. Red is training his two apprentices to be journeymen. When they have that experience and license, they will expect that level of pay. Right now, Red's does not have the marketing in place to attract enough customers to grow a company in just a few years that can support three journeymen and three apprentices on the job. This will require that Red remove himself from the plumbing

work and focus on the things that grow the company—like networking with contractors or bidding more jobs.

Getting Red into this role will help prevent the catastrophe that will
occur when the newly minted journeymen leave to work for the competitor who can and will gladly pay them what they deserve. Red's real
value to the company is not in doing the plumbing work. Instead, it is in
getting the work for others to do. In the marketing discussion in chapter
3, I addressed a list of the most common marketing strategies as follows:

- direct contact with existing customers
- networking and referral building
- public speaking
- writing and publicity
- promotional events
- advertising

Of these options, Red could easily be out working on the first two,
particularly if he chooses to focus on construction jobs more than residential service calls. Red's affability and experience makes this type of
marketing an easy path to business growth.

Advertising offers growth opportunities that could help Red keep
those journeymen and apprentices (who will be the next round of
growth for the company) in the field working. The problem is that
Red and Stephanie do not pay much attention to the world around
them, specifically the internet, and more particularly its impact on
marketing. Stephanie is aware of things like Amy's List—the web service that doles out recommendations for tradesmen—but she is too
busy minding the shop and raising the kids to give it much thought.

The internet completely changed the rules and possibilities of marketing and public relations.

7:1 Catastrophe in Sales

The point of marketing is to feed sales opportunities to the business. This is the point where you close the deal and sign the contract. It is that critical point where either your company has work to do or it does not. Red's has two types of sales: service calls and construction jobs.

The service-call customer typically has a disaster on their hands and needs the problem fixed immediately. These sales are easy to generate. The trick is to be there to answer the call and have someone on hand to do the work.

As with the lack of marketing, the lack of sales for construction jobs is a potential catastrophe for Red's. Construction jobs depend on relationships, because without a strong relationship with the contractors, they will not be calling your company for their jobs. Unless Red can implement better marketing strategies to include commercial construction jobs, his sales process is a catastrophe waiting to happen. It is not a catastrophe such as a natural disaster; in fact, it is unlikely that it will make Red and Stephanie go broke. However, we must keep everything in context, and Red and Stephanie want their business to grow and generate a larger income base for themselves and their family. The lack of a sales strategy is a brick wall that will prevent them from realizing their dreams.

Red's Plumbing Conclusion

On one hand, Red and Stephanie are like any mom-and-pop shop: they juggle many balls trying to make ends meet, and they dream a little along the way. What they have accomplished with their business is impressive; they made it further than most folks ever do. It took years of training, the guts to start their own business, and dedication to their customers to build the growing business they have. Beyond that, it has a solid foundation for them to build even more dreams on. It is worth a lot to them. The problem is that one drop of stupid can rob them of the life for which they have worked so hard and quash their dreams in the process.

On the other hand, they really can do better. The changes they need to make are not about being smart, but rather just about preventing stupid. I just outlined the ways that a catastrophe can destroy what they have or prevent them from getting what they want. The ounces of prevention are not difficult, but sometimes it takes an objective and experienced eye to see what the company needs. There is no reason that Red and Stephanie cannot learn how to analyze their business and its weaknesses. It is just a skill, like plumbing, fishing, skiing, or—more proverbially—riding a bike. Remember too that there is nothing new under the sun, so there are plenty of teachers out there to help them along the way.

In this chapter, I illustrated catastrophes and showed examples of how to use the BISR to set up the steps necessary to eliminate or prepare for them. These disasters come in many more forms than are initially obvious—from natural disasters to human-based errors, or the objective disasters. Then, there are the subjective catastrophes that depend on the owner's (or owners') plans for the business. These are harder to spot, and consequently can linger for years, slowly killing dreams and ambitions.

The BISR analysis of Red's Plumbing overlaps Catastrophe with the Ignorance and Ineptitude columns. You can see this in the overall weakness of Red's marketing system. The point of using the BISR is not to pigeonhole a problem into one of these categories but rather to identify it so you can ask the right questions about how to prevent or prepare for it. The usefulness of the BISR is in the dragnet effect it has on rooting out the existing and potential problems that can and may span multiple columns.

CHAPTER SUMMARY

- ✔ Red's Plumbing is an example of a typical small business where the owner has not prepared for catastrophe in the seven business systems.

- ✔ If Red does not address these possible catastrophes, his business will crumble.

- ✔ Red does not need to be smart to fix these problems. He only needs not to be stupid.

Ignorance in General

IGNORANCE AT ITS BASE IS A LACK OF KNOWLEDGE. THE SOLU-
tion to ignorance is education. Ignorance on your part, or on the part
of your employees, can kill or cripple your business. Not knowing how
to do the job right the first time can be certain death for your business.
Ignorance is a very expensive lesson to learn, both in out-of-pocket
and opportunity costs.

There are two kinds of ignorance: the ignorance you know about
and the ignorance you do not know about.

I call the first kind known ignorance. This is the easiest to deal
with, because you know what you (or your team) need to learn. When
I staffed my law firm, it had been a long while since I had had employees. I knew I was ignorant as an employer, or maybe I was simply rusty
about delegating work. I knew this was known ignorance, and thus
repairing this deficiency was easy. I immersed myself in reading management books and listening to audio files about delegation. My crash
course filled my brain with best practices. Now I knew what I had to
do, and with the resources available nowadays, I was able to get up to
speed quickly. Of course, I had plenty of issues along the way, but I

recognized the need to cure my ignorance, and I tackled the learning curve.

The other type of ignorance, the kind I call unknown ignorance, is much more problematic. There is another old saying, "You can't fix what you don't know is broken." This is the crux of unknown ignorance. Determining what you do not know is the biggest part of the struggle. Sometimes the best move you can make is to have an objective look at your business. Better yet is having a tool to examine the business so you can see where it is working and where it is not. That is why my firm uses the BISR to focus on the parts of a business that are not working well and to narrow down the reason for the failure, which frequently is ignorance.

With either known ignorance or unknown ignorance, the issue at hand is figuring out how to confront it. There are two ways: the easy way or the hard way.

I based the easy way on the principle I introduced early in this book: there is nothing new under the sun. When we face an ignorance point at my firm, I dust off the same statement every time: "If there's a problem in business, someone else has dealt with it before and written a book teaching us all about it. So, let's get the book and figure it out." The person who paid the price of that mistake and wrote a book about it gained the experience the *hard way*. The point of the easy way is to learn from those who have traveled this road before you so that you do not make that same mistake—and thus pay the price in a real-life, real-time disruption to your business.

Getting that education by figuring out what you need to learn and how to go about it is not always the easiest thing to do. I refer to yet another of my core principles, the piñata theory. If you pick up your stick and start smacking the piñata, you will be stunned at what you can learn. In this context, your "stick" is doing things like

- getting the Kindle app on your phone, downloading some relevant business books to read, and reading them;
- finding business podcasts or books on Audible to play on your commute or while driving between jobs;
- going to the business section at your local bookstore, picking some books, and, again, reading them;
- seeking out older, more experienced business owners, asking their advice, and then actually *listening* to them;
- getting a business coach to teach you to become more objective and make sound business decisions; or
- attending seminars on business subjects, where you can learn from the speakers as well as from the other attendees, who by natural self-selection are probably dealing with the same issues you are.

There is no absolute formula for how to achieve the knowledge you need, which is why I love the piñata theory so much. The idea is committing to learn whatever you need to know and following through. In the beginning, you may not know exactly what you need to learn, but in the words of the legendary Mick Jagger, "If you try sometimes, you just might find, you get what you need." It is funny how that works.

While we are on the subject of the easy way, it is important to remember to think for yourself. Gathering knowledge does not qualify you to put the pieces together to form a complete puzzle. Combining all your newfound knowledge into a functioning, profitable system is where wisdom comes in, and that requires experience. This is the line separating the rich from the broke. You must test your knowledge and make sure your system works and do so in ways that do not put everything you have built at risk. Running little controlled tests is the final stretch of the easy way of fixing ignorance.

In contrast to the easy way, which relies on recognizing ignorance and then taking active steps toward education and implementation, the hard way is without direction or purpose. Rather than proactively confronting your ignorance, the hard way is doing nothing and letting your ignorance fester until you destroy your business. The hard way is refusing to learn from your mistakes until the consequences get so painful that necessity forces you to learn or you go out of business.

Of course, the smart business owners take the easy way as much as possible, but every business owner has done things the hard way on more than one occasion. Part of this is because as you grow your skill set, you also grow your business. You are not going to learn every lesson the easy way. You will miss some ignorance points, because each time you and your business grow, you have a new devil at that level. This is why using the BISR is so useful (particularly to growing businesses), because repeated examination steers the business owner to ask the right questions that lead him or her to the easy way.

This is particularly critical because the lack of knowledge in any of the seven core systems can cripple or kill your business. Ignorance can strike any of the seven moving parts of your business at any time. Many small businesses start from scratch, based on a skill the owner has or a hobby he or she loves. Frequently, having a host of responsibilities in which the owner has no prior knowledge or experience overwhelms the new business owner. While the owner may be a genius in making a widget, he or she is often clueless about payroll, inventory control, accounts payable and receivable, and so forth. Thus, a rigorous analysis of what the owner does not know is paramount.

Next is the problem of employees. Hiring solid, reliable, trainable employees is the bane of many a small business. It is usually a constant struggle to train them, not only in the skill set required to do their jobs but also in how to function as a member of a team. All too frequently, you end up with that employee who just does not play well with others. Knowing who to hire and how to train them is a key skill set that the owner must know or outsource to a human resources firm.

Both the owner and the employees must dovetail into the company's production. Without solid knowledge about how to do the job on all levels, a company can quickly devolve into utter chaos. Many business owners do not understand the need for written procedures about how to do the work and the repeated training necessary to reinforce this. Education for employees, particularly given the fast changes that take place in today's economy, is essential. In addition, a business owner must know all about his or her vendors and their reliability. This is particularly true if the company's production relies on access to certain materials or on a limited number of sources for those materials.

Ignorance can also cause failures in a company's physical plant. I experienced this problem when I bought a stately old home in which to put my law firm. My problem was in not realizing how fast my business would grow. I was ignorant, and my having to search for a bigger office set us back several months.

Then there are the metrics, which business owners frequently have a difficult time understanding. That is presuming the business owner knew to get them done in the first place. Ignorance about what your profit-and-loss report, balance sheet, budget variance report, or other reports mean can seriously damage a company. Many small-business owners have no idea how to gather the information to generate these reports, let alone know how to decipher them. These numbers are the abstract representation of where your company is going. If you can read them, you will know at a glance whether you are doing great or headed to bankruptcy.

In marketing, a business owner needs to know who his or her customers are before they can be reached. This involves some market research, or education. Depending on your business, this process does not have to be a sophisticated one involving high-dollar outside firms. It can be as simple as asking questions like

- With whom would I like to work in terms of people and business?
- Who are they trying to reach?
- Can I make good money working for them?
- What common attributes can I recognize among these customers that I can then use to identify my preferred prospects?

When I started marketing my law firm, rather than just letting business wander in, those were the questions I asked myself. I always liked working with self-made mom-and-pop businesses or self-reliant, aggressive second- or third-generation owners of family businesses. I could identify with both because, though not in the same business as either of my parents, I come from a long line of independently minded business owners; and there is a good deal of overlap in clientele. Both kinds of businesspeople leave me feeling energized and inspired in my own business. Plus, they are making money, and so the blood-turnip rule does not apply.

It took some introspection, but I lost my ignorance by learning for whom I wanted to work. This did not solve the problem of how to get them in the door so I could dazzle them with our sales pitch. However, identifying the target helped me create a plan that quickly grew my business.

Sales works similarly, and if you are ignorant about what your customers want and are willing to pay for, you will have a great deal of difficulty. Understanding this can be a function of trial and error. Ask yourself why you did not make that sale, and then ask why you managed to do so on another occasion. Comparing those two scenarios is a good test case to educate yourself and your sales team about where your failures in sales are coming from.

Identifying and knowing how to fix a lack of knowledge in your business is critical to your success. It is an ongoing—in fact, never-ending—process, because even if you are not trying to grow your business, the world changes around you. If you are growing your business, the need for constant education and sound implementation is even more vital. There are always learning curves if you are running a business, but using the BISR helps determine not only what you need to tackle but also how steep those curves are, so you know how hard to apply yourself.

CHAPTER SUMMARY

✔ The ignorance of a business owner can kill the business.

✔ There are two types of ignorance: known and unknown.

✔ To address ignorance, a business owner should find sources that address his or her lack of knowledge: books, podcasts, mentors, seminars, and so forth.

Heather's Cupcakes:
A Case Study in Ignorance

JUST AS IN THE RED'S PLUMBING CASE WITH CATASTROPHES, the BISR provides a way to examine how a lack of knowledge can adversely affect a business. This time we will use another fictional business, Heather's Cupcakes. Here is what we know about this business:

- Heather is a happily married thirty-four-year-old woman with two kids in school. Her husband has a job and provides for most of the family's financial needs.
- Heather has always loved to cook, and desserts are her favorite.
- Her friends started asking her to make cakes and various baked treats for their family and for business parties.
- Heather liked the income and loved the work, so she decided to go into business five years ago.
- She got a loan for $50,000 and set up a small bakery and commercial kitchen in a strip mall near her home and her kids' school.
- Heather's Cupcakes is a limited liability company owned fifty-fifty by Heather and her husband.

- The company grossed $65,000 its last year in business and ran a 30 percent profit margin, and Heather was able to take home about a third of that.

- Heather hired her friend Jane, who also loves to bake, to work as part-time help six months ago.

- About 25 percent of the sales come from the small retail front that the shop has, and 75 percent comes from catering parties and special events.

- Heather's has a website that is classy, pretty, and has a good menu.

- Heather's is in a large city with serious growth potential, although there are several competitors.

- Heather does not have time for sales because she is busy running the current business and raising her kids.

- Heather would like to grow her company into a $250,000-a-year business so that she can buy a nicer home and help with the kids' college education.

- She would also like to have more opportunities to take vacations with the kids without worrying about lost revenue at the bakery.

Undoubtedly, Heather has had a substantial learning curve already. She has gone through her entrepreneurial spasm and hit the business world head-on. She has managed pretty well and is still standing. She has learned that making cupcakes and making money are two entirely different things. As the owner, she is responsible for all three roles of technician, manager, and entrepreneur, with a little help from her friend. Heather does not understand that she must delegate some of these three roles if she wants to grow her business.

Given what we know, here is how I would grade her Ignorance column in her BISR:

	2: IGNORANCE
1: Management	C
2: Personnel	C
3: Production	B
4: Plant	B
5: Metrics	C
6: Marketing	F
7: Sales	F

Figure 17: Ignorance Only: Heather's Cupcakes BISR

1:2 Ignorance in Management

Making the jump from a hobbyist to a successful business owner is a huge leap, and normally under these circumstances, I grade very low in the Management: Ignorance box. It takes serious commitment and dedication to tackle that learning curve. Heather is obviously a woman of considerable pluck, aptitude, and drive, and, as a result, the concern level goes down because she has already demonstrated her abilities.

However, unlike Red, who has Stephanie taking over most of the management functions, Heather does not have a wingman. She has many skills to learn regarding the other six core functions of her business. This gets her a C grade that might otherwise be a B, given her prior performance. Again, this is not a personal reflection on her; it is an indicator of her need to learn and grow so that her business can do well.

2:2 Ignorance in Personnel

The hiring of Jane is pretty telling on this front, because Heather hired a friend rather than an employee. It is the owner's job to know how to define the roles everyone in the company should play and to fill those with the right people. Very rarely does that include your friends.

One of many places that this situation can become a problem is in leadership and the ability to show the core mission of the company. Imagine if Jane did not grasp the time-honored maxim, "The customer is always right." Imagine the loss of business for Heather due to irate customers. Heather's business is a luxury business that attracts demanding customers that want things customized and done just so. If an employee does not understand this, and thus does not incorporate it in his or her treatment of the customers, the business is in for trouble. It is imperative that Heather's employees truly comprehend this; and when friends are involved, impressing such concepts can become problematic.

We had a similar situation at my firm once. One of my attorneys was concerned about the amount of time required for a project on which she was working. She was concerned that the bill was going to be too high because she had to reinvent the wheel in an area of law that was new to my firm, and we were unable to outsource the file. I knew right then that she did not grasp the core service that my firm provides, so I needed to explain it.

This type of education is essential for the employees of any company. They must understand the company's core mission, and they must know how to treat the customers. If the employees remain ignorant about this, the company will suffer. Performance will be weak. Customers will be unhappy. Product will be shoddy, and the overall operation will likely become a miserable place to work.

Having a firm, understandable company mission is, of course, a lot more important in service businesses or companies providing customized products than it is in a production-line venture. For example, if your team is putting together wooden toy cars or filling bags of beef jerky, it is more important for them not to be ignorant about how to put the wheels on or seal the bags than it is for them to know about the overall mission of the business.

3:2 Ignorance in Production

Heather only has one employee, so what should that employee's role entail? The first question to ask is, "What skill set does an employee at Heather's Cupcakes need?" Having spent my teenage years in the back of the local bakery as an assistant baker and dishwasher, I can offer the following:

- making batter
- baking cakes
- icing cakes
- cleaning the baking area
- doing the dishes

- serving customers
- delivering to parties and events
- setting up displays
- interacting with the events' hosts and making sure they are satisfied

This is a simple skill set. In Heather's case, making sure that the employees are not ignorant about their jobs centers on their ability to bake and finish a cake. This is not an altogether easy job. My old boss never let me get anywhere near the icing! It takes some skill and patience to turn out perfect sponge cakes. It takes an even higher degree of artistry to produce the beautiful cupcakes that Heather's demanding customers have come to expect.

It takes yet an even higher level of skill to generate the same quality and type of cupcakes consistently so that customer number two gets the same experience that customer number one got at her party just a few weeks ago. Making sure that the employees understand and implement the mission of a quality product is every bit as important as the mission of quality service.

4:2 Ignorance in the Physical Plant

Meanwhile, the team must have a place to work. Is Heather's location good? Will it inspire her target market? Will they be comfortable in the neighborhood?

If a retail front is part of the plan, it has to be attractive to customers. Heather needs both a retail side and a production or kitchen

area. Let's presume Heather is on top of this and has her store profes-
sionally decorated. She has some nice granite countertops and clean
display cases.

The nice retail shop is just half of the equation, because the real
work takes place in the baking room. It is hot and usually messy, with
flour and icing everywhere despite the best efforts to keep things tidy.
Heather wants to grow her business. Her space has just enough room
for a big mixer, an oven, and a four-by-eight worktable. These are close
quarters for an expanding business. It is likely that she will need to
find more space soon, and she should have thought this through, as
moving a business is time-consuming and expensive. Being knowl-
edgeable about the space needed to turn out the necessary volume of
product is a cornerstone of Heather reaching her goals.

5:2 Ignorance in Metrics

Measurements and metrics should come naturally to a baker, right?
Well, maybe. Heather is new to the business world. Frankly, like most
business owners, her shop grew out of her passion. She is getting to do
something that she loves and that has nothing to do with numbers;
rather, it is about selling little puffs of baked and iced love to smiling,
ecstatic customers. What could be better than that? Making a healthy
profit doing so would be better.

Starting on the bottom end, Heather needs to get a handle on her
costs per unit. Every one of those scrumptious little cupcakes has a
cost to Heather in ingredients, labor, and general overhead. She needs
to figure out what her cost is per cupcake so that she can then calculate

her profit on each one. Beyond that, she needs to have an idea of what the market will bear for her cupcakes. My educated guess is that it is a lot more than she thinks it is. To Heather, turning out a quality product is an everyday, commonplace, no-big-deal thing. To those grinning customers, though, it is magic that they are willing to pay for. This is especially true in a luxury business like Heather's. People are willing to pay good money for the experience.

Determining costs is just the start, however. Next, Heather needs to develop a forward-looking budget so that she can predict where her business will be in the future and set goals of where she wants to be. This is not a difficult task, but to keep the whole exercise from being just theory, she must test it weekly or monthly against a budget variance report that compares her budget to her actual expenditures. Then and only then will she start to see and understand whether her goals for her business match her reality. I can tell you from working with clients and from running my own firm, this little exercise is often one of the most sobering things a person will ever do.

Heather needs to be cognizant of a whole lot of other numbers going on in her business and start to measure them. The maxim here is, if you can measure it, you can manage it. For instance, if the strawberry cupcakes do not seem to be selling, Heather needs to record this and take note of what did and did not sell. Maybe it is time to open that spot for another tray of those lemon cupcakes that sell almost as quickly as she can bake them.

Heather can ascertain this information from the company's profit-and-loss sheet based on the categories of income that she has specified on it. For years, my shop did a bit of criminal defense for our existing clientele and their families. These cases were just little scrapes with the law. The problem was that the dramas these cases generated created substantial disruption to the office and detracted from our core mission of helping family-business owners.

I continued that line of work until one day I noticed on my profit-and-loss statement that criminal law generated only 4 percent of our income. Previously ignorant but no longer, the decision to drop that line immediately and completely was easy for me. I helped my firm and my clients and myself. The good news was that we did not miss the income, as we quickly made up the difference doing what we do best.

6:2 Ignorance in Marketing

Heather's has three types of customers: retail customers that buy from her storefront; nonbusiness customers that buy cupcakes for parties and so forth; and businesses that buy for their employees and customers.

Heather needs to determine whether she can effectively serve all three and make a profit doing so. She also needs to decide whom she wants to serve. She may not have an interest in the business customers. On the other hand, that may be where the revenue growth potential is. This is how the metrics tie to marketing.

The problem is that Heather has not yet considered these things. She created a business from her hobby but still has the mindset of a hobbyist rather than a businessperson. Her lack of revenue growth shows it. The retail trade in bakeries like hers is typically dependent on location. While Heather's has a decent location, she is not in a busy shopping mall. The party customers might provide good revenue, but reaching that market is probably a word-of-mouth enterprise, although the website might also be of help. In either the parties or the business sales, Heather's might want to market a "cupcake of the week club." This way she could generate repeat business, which cuts down on the time that Heather and her team must spend on sales. A business might love to access a cupcake service like this for either its employees or customers.

Heather has not thought this through. In fact, she has not thought about it much at all. This is a good time for the piñata theory. She needs to pick up her stick and start beating the piñata until she has some answers to these questions. Oddly enough, one of the best methods might be by binge-watching *Buddy's Bakery Rescue*, a TV show where Buddy, an expert in the baking business, goes into disastrously run bakeries and whips them into shape. Heather could learn a great deal about her business and would probably improve many of the other core systems of her business. This is an example of using whatever expertise is available to reduce your ignorance and increase your knowledge.

7:2 Ignorance in Sales

Heather's sales mirror her marketing in that there are three customer types. The retail sales are easy: "I'd like a dozen cupcakes." Then the customer selects those that they want and either Heather or her employee packages them in a tasteful Heather's Cupcakes' box.

Even the party sales are simple. The customers are primed. They come to the bakery ready to put on a special event, and Heather's has just the cupcakes they need to enhance their entertaining prowess.

The business sales are a bit more of a challenge. In the preceding section, I mentioned the idea of a subscription program. That might be a way for Heather to break into business sales. However, Heather has yet to consider her possible marketing strategies. In thinking about my own business, I would love to send the new members of our General Counsel Subscription Program a couple dozen special cupcakes, and if Heather were engaged in active marketing, I would know just whom I needed to call to implement this plan.

Unfortunately, Heather has not explored ways to expand beyond the retail and party sales opportunities. That may be all she needs to do, based on the proliferation of cupcake stores across the country. Again, the sales correspond closely to marketing because marketing brings in the opportunities.

Heather's Cupcakes Conclusion

The stalling of Heather's business is a direct result of Heather's lack of knowledge in marketing and sales. She has already demonstrated the ability to produce. Now, she needs to develop her procedures and recipes to ensure consistent quality. With the increased customer demand, she also needs to make sure she has the properly trained staff on board and that they support her service mission. Without the increase in business, however, none of this matters.

With the increase of cupcake stores nationally and Heather's market in a large city, this should be possible. The former tells us that there is aggregate demand. It also may indicate market saturation, but that might simply mean that the customers are primed; and there is always room at the top in any market. Presuming Heather's quality is top-notch, she just needs to get the word out and close some sales. Her ignorance in this vital aspect of business is her problem.

Marketing and sales help are essential for this company to grow. Heather has a lot on her plate with her business and her family. If she continues to work on the production and employee systems herself and brings in a business consultant or perhaps an experienced salesperson, Heather has a very good chance at achieving her business goals.

CHAPTER SUMMARY

✔ Many people turn their craft into a business, but those people are not necessarily ready to be entrepreneurs.

✔ In order to grow, these craftsmen-turned-bosses need to look at their seven systems of business.

Ineptitude in General

————

INEPTITUDE IS WHEN YOU KNOW WHAT YOU NEED TO DO IN your business and are either not doing it or not making sure someone is doing it right. The correction for this problem is in many ways the least complex and yet the most difficult to achieve. The human factor that we try to control using checklists, workflows, and systems is what makes it so. We as humans get lazy, inattentive, and careless. We forget, overlook, or skip steps in the job necessary for a business to run successfully. When these situations create a problem for a business, when the team knows what they should be doing but don't do it, this is ineptitude.

The counterintuitive element of ineptitude is that it is more prevalent in established operations than it is in smaller, newer businesses. The reasons for this vary and can range from businesses resting on their laurels to failure to train new employees. These established companies have so much internal intelligence that many have forgotten more than most other companies will ever know. Then they get lazy based on their success. Someone in the operation becomes complacent, and then the stupid mistakes happen.

I know how this happens because I have been there. We have several clients whom I have worked with for so long, we are like peas and carrots. We have tried the "same" cases dozens of times to judges and arbitrators. We know the cases inside and out and use the same exhibit format every time, because it all works like clockwork. That is, except for the time we messed up Exhibit 3.

When preparing for these cases, typically we divided the preparation work between our client and our staff. Once, some of the underlying calculations we received from our client were way off. This effectively damaged our calculations and pretty much the whole case. In short, our case was a mess and the arbitrator caught it. Neither my client's assistant manager nor my office caught the discrepancy. Although we had not previously seen this problem in our firm, it was an obvious place for a problem to occur in the case. Fortunately, we made a quick recovery on that case, and more importantly, we put safeguards—in the form of checklists—in place in both of our operations to make sure that it never happened again.

Our protocols are simple enough. On each end we double-check the numbers. I have in my checklist how to prepare a case like this, and my client double-checks his assistant manager's work. To control ineptitude, build in systems and checklists that ensure your team fulfills all the steps required for the job. This fail-safe can prevent disasters from happening to your business.

Pilots execute a very complicated checklist before they take off because flying is a complex operation filled with pitfalls that can have deadly consequences. Yet the incidents of accident are miniscule. Your chances of dying in a car wreck are much greater than they are of dying on a commercial flight. The reason for this is an absolute intolerance for ineptitude. Authorities require pilots and crew to go through their extremely detailed checklists every time, including the annoying reminder of how to fasten a seat belt! The use of these systems and checklists is what makes flying so safe.

I previously mentioned *The Checklist Manifesto*. The study that spurred the writing of that book involved operating rooms at hospitals around the world, ranging from topflight clinics in America to rudimentary hospitals in rural Africa. The experiment introduced detailed checklists for the surgical team to follow so that they were not operating from memory. The results were amazing, even among the highly skilled surgeons in the best hospitals where previously bad results had occurred. If a simple checklist can make such a remarkable difference in life-and-death situations conducted by highly skilled professionals who have done the same job many times before, what kind of difference could the implementation of checklists make in your business?

The answer is a remarkable difference. Additionally, there is a bonus in that the owner no longer must explain how to do the job and then double-check constantly to make sure the employees correctly complete the entire process. Checklists can lift massive burdens off the shoulders of a business owner in both time and stress.

A checklist is just one way of controlling ineptitude. It is the baseline way of making sure your employees follow the correct procedures. It may not always be the best way of teaching those steps, however. If I put a checklist in front of a young lawyer explaining how to put together a case or a transaction, they are likely to roll their eyes in apprehension and dread. They may have learned how to do these tasks in law school, but doing them in the real world is completely different.

I know that this situation spans the gap between ignorance and ineptitude, so we deal with it in a different way: we teach novice lawyers how to do it by using Jing videos—or, for the Apple users, Screenflow. We primarily use Jing to take videos of working screenshots, with audio, of how to prepare all the common documents in our office. It consists of an instructor pulling up the document form in question, turning on the Jing video recorder, and then explaining how to cut, paste, edit, and wrap up the document. This allows the viewer to see how to create these documents with a detailed instruction by an expert. It is an effective tool, not only to educate but also to refresh memories and systematize the office. Backed up with the checklist, you have a solid cover for ineptitude.

Ben Franklin really nailed this when he said, "Tell me and I forget, teach me and I may remember, involve me and I will learn." I would add one more thing to Franklin's quote: "Remind me and I will do it right." We all get lackadaisical in our jobs. Even things that were once new and exciting bore people. Human error is the most common reason for business failures. This a controllable issue, and business owners must be diligent to stem ineptitude.

Ineptitude may sound more benign than ignorance, but the result is the same—the failure to get the job done right. The results of failures caused by ineptitude can be every bit as devastating or embarrassing to a business owner as those caused by ignorance. The result is frequently the same and can be costly. The good news about ineptitude is that it is usually easier to control, because you already know what the problem is. It may be more annoying and tedious, but at least you know the demon you are dealing with, because you already know how to do the job right.

The issues are basic: train your employees and then make sure that they follow through. This is not always the easiest job in the world. It can get even worse if they perceive you are being bossy and condescending, particularly if you have a shop of skilled employees, such as electricians, carpenters, or—even worse—lawyers. Under these circumstances, preventing ineptitude becomes as much a question of leadership as of just knowing how to do the job right.

The human factor is more complicated than it may seem at first. You can tell your employees, show them, involve them, and even remind them and they still may do exactly what and how they please. Short of termination, the solution to get your employees to follow your procedures is ultimately a question of leadership, and no one addresses this better than John Maxwell in his book *The 5 Levels of Leadership*.

We really only need the first two levels of leadership, which are positional and permissive. Someone who has positional leadership has the leadership role by virtue of his or her position. It may be because they own the company. It may be because the owner named them the manager. Regardless, this person has a leadership position, and some people will follow them by virtue of their position. The problem is there are some people who will not follow their leader, due to reasons ranging from lack of respect for the position (or of the person in the position) to outright intransigence. This then becomes a personnel problem.

Alternatively, a positional leader can grow to be a permissive leader. This does not refer to a leader who is permissive—one who lets the employees do whatever they want. In fact, in this case, "permissive" applies to the employees, who give permission to be led. It involves the leader gaining the trust of the employees and then taking them in a direction that benefits the team (and thus the company). It involves a degree of likability and good faith on the part of the leader to be able to communicate well with the team and create a shop environment where everyone is operating on the same page and with the same goal. Business owners can only reach the goal of avoiding the mistakes of ineptitude when they have permissive leaders in place; this is so that your team is willing to comply with the rules, directives, checklists, and workflows that prevent ineptitude from striking your business. With ineffective leadership, this willingness is probably not going to occur. However, if you set the culture just right and your managers follow through, your business can be productive and profitable.

The impact of ineptitude can affect the most practical parts of a business, such as the physical plant. People commonly forget to renew the insurance on their building and equipment. The same sort of issues might arise in relation to safety equipment. Simple things like making sure the fire extinguishers are in place and in working order can easily escape proper attention. If you have a small fire and someone uses the fire extinguisher, do you remember to refill it? Fire alarm batteries are another example. If the fire alarm starts going off because it senses a low battery, it is common for people to just remove the battery and place it back up there. In the realm of ineptitude, this type of situation strikes all too often. When you need the alarm, it is too late to put in a new battery.

Your company's policies, systems, and procedures are the front line of defense against ineptitude and at the same time are one of the primary areas where you will see ineptitude in action. That seems a little counterintuitive, doesn't it? The problem stems from human nature and the aversion to sitting down and writing out the policies. Even I, who preach about, live by, and recognize the necessity of written procedures, hate writing them down when I know I need to do so. Worse yet is knowing that a written policy in your business does not work and failing to update it.

The failure either to create procedures when you know you need them or to fix the ones you know are not working is the pinnacle of ineptitude. In the early stages of growth at Davis Law, we had some real problems with our delegation procedures. The bottom line was that my senior associate and I were not communicating well with the junior associates, whom we had divided into teams. They were cranky and dissatisfied with their jobs. These were high achievers—top-notch new lawyers—who excelled throughout college and law school. They wanted to rock the law business, and my systems were failing them. To make matters worse, I knew better. I knew that the system was not working. I only partially documented the system, and it was inadequate. Because I am well aware of the importance of writing such procedures down, I forced myself to accomplish the task. Yes, it was annoying and tedious, but that is what it takes to run a successful business, and if you do it right, you can make a lot more money, because you have fewer mistakes. Ultimately, I came to love writing the procedures, because I saw that they were a vehicle to teaching my team how to do our work and to do it right, which saves me time and money.

Metrics are also the bane of many a business owner. The person who loves math and keeping track of it in an ongoing business is a rare find. For that math lover to be the same person as the business owner is even rarer, because the entrepreneurial personality type has that bit of dreamer who tends to avoid details. Thus, we spring the trap of metrics ineptitude. The moral to the story is when you find that person who loves the details and can work with your team—keep them happy!

Ineptitude manifests itself in a company's measurements in raw, unkempt neglect, and it can be deadly. If a company does not keep track of its costs or its expenditures, pretty soon it will be in the red. You can operate without a forward-looking budget, without cash-flow reports, and without the other reports that you should have, but doing so is leaving you blind not only to the financial risks of your business but also to the growth opportunities. Sometimes it is being aware of the simple numbers of your business that can make all the difference.

Recently, I decided not to hire another attorney and let my firm remain at its given size until my chief financial officer confronted me. I always know the revenue capacity of my firm because I keep track of all the lawyers' time weekly. Beyond that, I know how many hours we can routinely put in every month. My CFO pointed out how close we were coming to maximum capacity each month. In short, she pointed out that I was ineptly looking at the numbers that I already knew! Duly chastened, I got my ad ready for the bar journal.

Marketing is also a place where ineptitude can hamstring your business, but it is a curious one. What distinguishes ineptitude from catastrophe and ignorance is the presumption that you already know what to do but don't do it, thereby causing problems in your business—and in this case your marketing. Most business owners do not have a solid grasp of their ideal customer, and thus they do not know how to begin marketing their business. The result of this is that they never really market because they have not identified whom they want to serve.

Instead, they spend their efforts in things such as getting general exposure by buying an eight-by-twelve-foot ad on the outfield wall of the local ballpark or running a general yellow pages ad. They do not focus on bringing the right customers into their marketing funnel; rather, they put their time and money into "just getting my name out there." That may work in some instances, but it is not optimal. I know because I have lived it. General ads in the law business lead to endless calls from people who want to shop for the lowest-price-of-entry retainer, rather than for the best fit for their problem. Many of those calls do not result in actual paying clients. I briefly tried general advertising, until I realized I was better off not being in the phone book at all and that I was instead better off relying on word of mouth to bring in reasonably good clients. This is not true for all business types, however.

Sales has some of the same elements of human nature that marketing does and thus has similar pitfalls in closing the deal. Naturally, not every customer is the same, and regardless of the beneficial value proposition that your goods or services can provide, you will not get the same response from one potential client to another. You cannot control this, but you can perfect your pitch to bring in the largest volume of the right customers for your business.

Another level of ineptitude in sales is becoming so overconfident about your company that you forget to listen. A good salesperson, whether a dedicated one or just a member of the team, can convince customers to tell them what they want; the key is asking the right questions and then listening to their response. Unfortunately, many companies have people running their sales discussion who are so impressed with how successful they are or how awesome their company is that they forget to listen to the customer. This sort of ineptitude is how many great opportunities die.

Ineptitude may have the worst sting of all the types of failure because of the "I already knew better" factor. It is the most vexing because one aspect of it is that it should be easy to control, because the knowledge already exists. The problem lies in following through and doing what is necessary or having a team that can and will take care of the issues plaguing your company. Because of the human factor, ineptitude is going to happen. It is going to happen repeatedly. However, the use of the BISR is a sound tool to reduce its intensity and frequency—and even eliminates some of those problems altogether.

CHAPTER SUMMARY

✓ Ineptitude is when you know what you need to do in your business and are either not doing it or not making sure someone does it correctly.

✓ To control ineptitude, one must create systems and checklists that ensure the team completes all tasks necessary for a job well done.

✓ Lists and systems alleviate burden from the owner, who no longer must micromanage every task to guarantee its correct completion.

✓ Leaders can be positional, permissive, or both.

Johnson's Hardware:
A Case Study in Ineptitude

———

BECAUSE INEPTITUDE IS MORE COMMON IN ESTABLISHED businesses, we are going to examine an imaginary business quite a bit older than Red's Plumbing and Heather's Cupcakes combined. Let us call it Johnson's Hardware. Stan Johnson took over when his father, Larry, died. Larry started the hardware store sixty years ago, while in his late forties, when he decided that he no longer enjoyed life on the road as a traveling sales representative. At the time, his son, Stan, was a bit of a troubled teen, and Larry decided that his family needed him at home.

The plan worked, and Stan straightened up and attended the local college. He did pretty well, graduating in just over four years. Stan then joined his father in the business. They ran it together for thirty years, with Larry taking a back seat early on because he was fairly pleased with his son's acumen. He also appreciated the free time his son's involvement afforded him—time to pursue other pleasures, such as joining his cohorts at the diner for coffee and gossip. This scenario brings us up-to-date with Stan, now in his mid-seventies, and his hands still firmly on the reins.

The store started in a classic downtown of a nice country town on the edge of a fast-growing city. Over the past sixty years, the city engulfed the town, and now it is a suburb. The downtown retained its character and is now a thriving little avenue full of boutique shops and restaurants. Johnson's Hardware remained a cornerstone shop by providing service with a smile and convenience for those who prefer not to fight the crowds at the big-box stores. Stan has weathered many changes and is fairly open-minded for a man his age, a necessity for the long-term success of a business.

In fact, the store became such a local fixture that with the encouragement of his wholesaler, Stan took over the operations of two locations of a failed competitor in neighboring suburbs. So, Stan is riding out what could be his retirement running three locations and loving it!

Here are the relevant data points on the stores:

- The main store is nine thousand square feet, with adequate parking, and was paid for long ago.
- Stan's wife has no interest in the business and never has.
- He has no kids in the business and no successor in place.
- The shop has had a series of clerks in and out of it.
- Stan has a grandson in college who is working at the store part-time, and he would like to hand the business over to him one day, if he is interested, but Stan has not talked to him about it.
- About twenty years ago, Stan merged the shop into the True Value Hardware network so that he operates somewhat like a franchisee, with True Value providing significant guidance and some direction in the running of his stores.

- The two other stores have managers that Stan "inherited" when he took over those locations. Both are in their sixties and still operate their shops by the rules that were in place before Stan bought them, because Johnson's does not have written policies and procedures in place except for a rudimentary employee handbook.
- The shopping experience at each Johnson's Hardware is very different. The main location is tidy and cheery, while the other locations exhibit indifference to cleanliness and customer service.
- Each store has between five and seven employees, including the manager.
- Stan still works as the manager of the original location.
- The revenue is $1.2 million per year on a profit margin of 10 percent.
- This is over and above Stan's annual salary of $60,000.
- The shop has used the same accountant for the past forty years. He is a friend of Stan's from church and softball league when they were young.
- About ten years ago, the accountant talked Stan into incorporating the business so that he could elect as an S corporation and take the profits as dividends.
- Stan sponsors a local Little League ball team every year.
- Johnson's Hardware carries consumer goods and hardware items.
- The other line of business is in white goods—refrigerators, washers, dryers, dishwashers, and so forth.
- Stan knows that the white-goods sales have been on the rise in recent years, but he does not know by how much and has not taken steps to market them, even though he knows he could grow that aspect of his business.

	3: INEPTITUDE
1: Management	C
2: Personnel	C
3: Production	B
4: Plant	B
5: Metrics	C
6: Marketing	D
7: Sales	B

Figure 18: Ineptitude Only: Johnson's Hardware BISR

1:3 Ineptitude in Management

To begin with, Stan knows that he needs a successor. He just does not want to think about it. He encouraged his kids to go on to college and build a better life, rather than just being a "shopkeeper." Of course, the irony of this is that he loves his shop, his customers, and his everyday life as a shopkeeper. Unfortunately, his devotion to the shops kept him from training someone to replace him. While this puts the business in a position of vulnerability in the catastrophic event of him dying, it falls into the realm of ineptitude because he already knows that he needs a successor in place.

Stan also knows that he is the boss and thus that he needs to shake things up at the other stores. However, he does not want to go to the trouble of firing the managers who have run those shops since before he bought them. He is reluctant to go to the other locations because it irritates him to see the inefficiency rampant there, but he refuses to make the necessary personnel changes because he does not want to upset the apple cart. Stan's reservations about providing real business leadership for the company are a classic form of ineptitude, where misplaced loyalty and the refusal to make sound business decisions adversely affect business performance as well as growth.

2:3 Ineptitude in Personnel

This ineptitude pours over to how the employees act in the business. As is true in most things, the problems start at the top, and businesses reflect what is going on in the owner's head. The managers know they are adrift. On one hand, they kind of like their independence, but on the other hand, they are uninspired by their jobs. Johnson's is not a place with a culture that encourages innovation and excellence. The original location is, but the integration of the new stores did not follow that good example.

Stan is displaying ineptitude in leadership by not getting a team together. The problem is that Stan never built a team. He just took the new stores over without any experience in leadership beyond running the original location, so he lets the other stores run on autopilot.

Fortunately for Stan, hardware stores are not a highly regulated industry. When a business has governmental rules they must abide by, the possibility of the employees failing to comply even though they know the regulations makes the problems from ineptitude a lot more common. Still, Stan has his share of frustration with his employees, who are not even managing their main responsibilities of tending the shops and providing customer service.

3:3 Ineptitude in Production

Johnson's is fortunate to be a part of the True Value chain, because they take care of identifying what inventory should be in the shops. True Value has nationwide experience and sophistication. Despite watching how this organization streamlines the stores, Stan has fought suggestions from both the True Value representatives and his accountant to develop internal policies and procedures for his stores. Instead, he chooses to rely on his managers to run their own shops. This leads to each location of Johnson's Hardware having its own identity. You might as well be shopping at a completely different company when you go between the Johnson's locations. This causes customers a problem. If store number one is out of a product, then the employees should be able to send customers to store number two. Unfortunately, this is not the case at Johnson's Hardware.

4:3 Ineptitude in the Physical Plant

Stan is a man without a plan and his shops reflect this failure. He realizes that it would benefit his business to update the two other locations. The original location succeeds on its small-town charm, but that does not translate into success for the two modern-style retail stores. In addition, the other locations do not have Stan and the customer loyalty that he has garnered over the years. The sales are slumping because the competition is meeting the customer's needs with available inventory, clean shops, and good customer service. The solution to Stan's problems is not difficult. An investment of perhaps $50,000 per location would make all the difference, and Stan knows it. The problem is that he is adrift, resting on his past successes and doing what he really loves—helping customers.

5:3 Ineptitude in Metrics

Stan's metrics are in place, and he has a solid accountant. Still, he does not feel like he is getting ahead. That $3 million nest egg that he wanted to have by this time in his life is not there. He knows that he should pay closer attention to the numbers, but he is complacently focusing on the day-to-day pleasure of helping his customers find just the right widget. He knows this lack of attention is a key source of his failure to achieve his financial goals. Stan's refusal to use his numbers to take advantage of the opportunities available to him with his three locations reflects his ineptitude in metrics.

6:3 Ineptitude in Marketing

The question of what Stan could further do to market his business is an interesting one. All three stores have the "corner store" appeal and serve the local customer base well. There are competitors, but they do not seem to be putting a dent in the original business, whereas the other Johnson's locations have begun to lose customers. Stan's customers are mainly routine retail-trade walk-ins that need a lawn mower blade or a can of paint. Because Johnson's original location offers personal service and convenience—in contrast to the big-box stores—the growing aversion many consumers have developed for the big-box stores is an advantage for Stan's shop.

Still, Stan has not taken any action to step up his marketing. While the trend of shopping local plays well into Stan's opportunities to sell more white goods, and he can see the upward sales trend in his financials, he is not doing anything about it. He believes his Little League baseball sponsorships, which have always worked to bring in customers, will continue to do so, despite the current demographics showing that soccer is growing and that the soccer moms buy the white goods. In short, we have a stable business, but not one that is maximizing its opportunities. Evidently, Stan is happy where he is.

7:3 Ineptitude in Sales

Sales at Johnson's are the routine business of consumer transactions. The key to them is solid customer service. Stan has a long-term workforce, but it is not clear whether they really understand how to help a customer who comes in needing a new hinge for his or her gate. The bottom line is Stan has not paid any attention to customer service. He figures it will take care of itself. Oddly enough, based on the company's stability, it seems to have done just that.

Johnson's Hardware Conclusion

Johnson's Hardware is a business on autopilot. Through two generations, the company has done well enough to take over a competitor.

At this point, however, it is stagnant and will begin to atrophy if the next business trend to come along does not give the advantage to Johnson's the way the trend away from big-box stores has. If the next trend is in the growth of online retailers like Amazon, Johnson's could be in trouble. Stan's customers appreciate the convenience of the small local store with the friendly face; however, buying from your smartphone could very well trump that.

Then there is the real head-scratcher of Stan's age, with no retirement in sight. His life has been the business. Yet, he cannot even bring himself to prepare to hand it over to his grandson, let alone discuss it with him to find out whether the young man is even interested. It is a glaring oversight on Stan's part and he knows it.

This is a business with great potential, provided it has some leadership. Perhaps this grandson is the right one for the job. There are plenty of points of ineptitude making the company vulnerable, including the two over-sixty managers at the other store. This tired company needs new life, and the lackadaisical attitude speaks volumes.

CHAPTER SUMMARY

- ✓ Johnson's Hardware is an example of a business that has survived long-term as a cornerstone community business but is not seeing the growth in profit that it should.

- ✓ The stagnation of businesses like Stan's is due to leadership ineptitude.

- ✓ To combat these issues, Stan must take initiative as illustrated in the piñata theory.

Conclusion

———

UNDERSTANDING THE NATURE AND ORIGINS OF PROBLEMS IS critical to your success. I started this book by outlining the subjective nature of problems because it is vital for you to grasp that your business goals set the stage for your business problems. In fact, as I stated earlier, they are two sides of the same coin. This book will help you identify your goals so that you can begin to prepare for the potential threats to them.

As a second step in this process, we ventured into where these threats originate in the systems that work behind the scenes. Part of this was to introduce the idea that there is a "right" way for a business to work. Still, this "right" way is an elusive concept until you examine it in the light of practicality, legality, and morality. By using the metaphor of how a body's immune system works, I laid the groundwork for introducing the concept of the Business Immune System.

Then I introduced you to the actual seven working parts of every business. This portion of the book illustrated that all businesses, from the smallest to the largest, operate with the same seven systems. These systems vary from business to business, but their proper functioning for the given business and its goals determines the success or failure of every business. This is where the understanding of problems and their origins started to get real. This gave us a list of systems to start to build out the methodology to examine where potential problems might arise.

Next came the idea of adding the eighth system—the one designed to protect all the others. In this chapter, I used metaphor to illustrate how this system acts like our body's immune system to prevent or react to threats posed to the proper functioning of the core systems. I stressed the importance of having the proactive defenses in place, because fixing problems is much more expensive than preventing them.

The final piece was to incorporate the three ways that businesses fail to protect themselves. All business failures are a result of three things: the inability to prevent or prepare for catastrophe, the toleration of ignorance, or the acceptance of ineptitude. These three failure symptoms, when cross-referenced with the seven working parts, build the framework of the Preventing Stupid Method by outlining the necessary questions to construct your Business Immune System.

With the structure in place, I explained how to build your BIS. It is an art, not a science. It is dependent on your goals, the goods or services that you sell your labor market, and a host of other factors. This process also includes prioritizing the threats most likely to materialize (or at least those that could cause the most serious damage to your business). In short, I stressed your role as the subjective hub around which the entire enterprise must turn.

Considering the daunting task of building your BIS from scratch, I gave you my standard pep talk. I pointed out that successful business owners have accomplished this process many, many times before. I stressed the need to "pick up your stick" and start trying to crack open the piñata. Finally, I revisited my favorite fable to underscore that diligence, not brilliance, is the key to building a successful BIS.

From here, we homed in on catastrophes in the abstract. Again, there are the ones that are acts of God. Even more insidious than these natural disasters are the human ones. To add yet a further twist is the fact that you—yes, you—are one of the two types of human catastrophes. The other type is whomever your business deals with, ranging from employees to vendors to regulators.

Taking this analysis of catastrophes, we looked at Red's Plumbing to see the disasters for which they failed to prepare. By walking through the seven systems, we found quite a few. Having already learned the basic principles of the Preventing Stupid Method, you were probably not surprised at the ease of fixing most of Red and Stephanie's vulnerabilities. Likewise, I hope you were able to discern how effective the BISR is in identifying them.

Next, I discussed ignorance in its two forms—known and unknown. I addressed several ways that you could seek out education to resolve ignorance. In fact, lifelong learning is the key to preventing stupid, avoidable errors from ruining your business.

Heather's Cupcakes provided the vehicle for examining how ignorance can pose threats to a business. I chose Heather because she recently started her business and because she, as a hobbyist-turned-budding-entrepreneur, has a lot to learn about running a successful company. Again, there is no shame in not knowing, but there is great shame in not trying to learn. Her example represents common scenarios of what a startup business goes through before it really begins to prosper.

In the final abstract chapter, I delved into ineptitude. This is perhaps the most insidious and painful way to fail, because the solution is right in front of you. Thus, not only does the problem hurt, but so too does your pride, because ineptitude frequently involves a failure of leadership. I addressed the best preventive measures, which include solid operating procedures, checklists, and processes.

In contrast to Heather's, I examined ineptitude in a sixty-year-old business, Johnson's Hardware. There, Stan Johnson had been and continued to be successful—perhaps not as successful as he could have been, but well enough to suit him at the time. We identified issues within his business that required action to ensure the long-term viability of his business. For reasons ranging from indifference to laziness, he chose to tolerate those problems. That is his prerogative and, unfortunately, one that you see all too often in businesses of that age.

My goal is to help you run as effective and trouble-free a business as possible. A key to doing this is to understand the necessity of routinely running an effective risk analysis of your business. The Preventing Stupid Method provides the tools you need to accomplish this task. It covers all the working systems of your business and the three ways you can fail. The twenty-one categories this process creates outline a comprehensive list of smart questions to ask yourself so that you can ward off the threats to your business.

As you ask these questions, identify the threats, and then develop the preventive or reactive solutions, your BIS begins to come together. What were once "that was a stupid mistake" moments turn into "okay, we're prepared for this" moments that result in more money in your bank account, because you can focus on productive work rather than just putting out fires. That is where I want you to be, and I hope my Preventing Stupid Method will help you get there.

So, quit being stupid, and go forth and prosper!

Quick Reference Guide

THIS QUICK REFERENCE GUIDE PROVIDES YOU WITH WORK-sheets to begin your process of evaluating your business systems. Using the lessons learned in *The Art of Preventing Stupid* and the sample business stories, complete the blank worksheets by entering your own business information.

EXAMPLE 1: BUSINESS IMMUNE SYSTEM REPORT: FAILURE EXAMPLES

BUSINESS IMMUNE SYSTEM REPORT: FAILURE EXAMPLES			
	CATASTROPHE	**IGNORANCE**	**INEPTITUDE**
Management	Owner Is Disabled in Car Wreck	Owner Does Not Know Key Skill Set	Owner Has Not Preserved Cash for Payday
Personnel	Key Person Dies	Team Does Not Have Required Skills	Owner Has Overlooked Key Job Function
Production	Computers or Registers Crash	Team Is Improperly Trained	Job Functions Are Repeatedly Performed Incorrectly
Plant	Fire Burns Down Plant	Company Has Purchased Wrong Size of Building	Rent Is Not Paid on Time
Metrics	Major Data Loss due to Computer Crash	Good Tax Strategy Not Developed	Company Has Failed to Maintain Measurements on Production
Marketing	Horrible Press due to Car Wreck by Driver	Key Customers Not Identified	Reaching Out to Wrong Customers
Sales	Key Meeting Is Missed by Salesperson	Salesperson Is Not Prepared to Answer Key Objections to a Deal	Failure to Call Customers Back

WORKSHEET 1

BUSINESS IMMUNE SYSTEM REPORT: FAILURE EXAMPLES			
	CATASTROPHE	IGNORANCE	INEPTITUDE
Management			
Personnel			
Production			
Plant			
Metrics			
Marketing			
Sales			

NOTES:

_____

_____

_____

_____

_____

_____

EXAMPLE 2: BUSINESS PROBLEM SEVERITY SCALE

	SAMPLE BUSINESS PROBLEM SEVERITY SCALE
1	Hot Check
2	Small Unpaid Receivable
3	Small Lost Customer
4	Bad Press
5	Small-Claims Suit
6	Loss of Key Employee
7	Bankruptcy Reorganization
8	Major Lawsuit
9	Insolvency
10	Liquidation

WORKSHEET 2

	SAMPLE BUSINESS PROBLEM SEVERITY SCALE
1	
2	
3	
4	
5	
6	
7	
8	
9	
10	

NOTES:

EXAMPLE 3: THE FOUR TYPES OF PROBLEMS: BUSINESS VERSION

THE FOUR TYPES OF PROBLEMS: BUSINESS EXAMPLE		
	FIXABLE	NON-FIXABLE
Preventable	Unpaid (but Collectible) Receivable	Data Loss with No Backup
Non-Preventable	Other Party Destroys a Key Vehicle or Machine	Owner Dies in a Catastrophe

WORKSHEET 3

THE FOUR TYPES OF PROBLEMS: BUSINESS EXAMPLE		
	FIXABLE	NON-FIXABLE
Preventable		
Non-Preventable		

EXAMPLE 4: MANAGEMENT METHODS OF THE FOUR TYPES OF PROBLEMS

MANAGEMENT METHODS OF THE FOUR TYPES OF PROBLEMS		
	FIXABLE	**NON-FIXABLE**
Preventable	Prevent	Prevent and Protect
Non-Preventable	Protect	Protect

WORKSHEET 4

MANAGEMENT METHODS OF THE FOUR TYPES OF PROBLEMS		
	FIXABLE	**NON-FIXABLE**
Preventable		
Non-Preventable		

NOTES:

_____

_____

_____

_____

EXAMPLE 5: BISR SAMPLE

BUSINESS IMMUNE SYSTEM REPORT: FAILURE EXAMPLES		
	CATASTROPHE	IGNORANCE	INEPTITUDE
Management	A	D	A
Personnel	F	C	C
Production	A	A	A
Plant	A	A	A
Metrics	A	C	A
Marketing	A	D	A
Sales	A	C	A

WORKSHEET 5

BUSINESS IMMUNE SYSTEM REPORT: FAILURE EXAMPLES		
	CATASTROPHE	IGNORANCE	INEPTITUDE
Management			
Personnel			
Production			
Plant			
Metrics			
Marketing			
Sales			

NOTES:

_____

_____

_____

EXAMPLE 6: CATEGORIES OF CATASTROPHES

CATEGORIES OF CATASTROPHES			
	NATURAL	HUMAN	INTERNAL
Objective			
Subjective			

WORKSHEET 6

CATEGORIES OF CATASTROPHES			
	NATURAL	HUMAN	INTERNAL
Objective			
Subjective			

NOTES:

_____

_____

_____

_____

_____

EXAMPLE 7: CATASTROPHE ONLY: RED'S PLUMBING BISR

CATASTROPHE ONLY: BUSINESS IMMUNE SYSTEM REPORT	
	1: CATASTROPHE
1: Management	C
2: Personnel	C
3: Production	B
4: Plant	B
5: Metrics	C
6: Marketing	F
7: Sales	F

WORKSHEET 7

CATASTROPHE ONLY: BUSINESS IMMUNE SYSTEM REPORT	
	1: CATASTROPHE
1: Management	
2: Personnel	
3: Production	
4: Plant	
5: Metrics	
6: Marketing	
7: Sales	

NOTES:

_____

_____

_____

EXAMPLE 8: IGNORANCE ONLY: HEATHER'S CUPCAKES BISR

IGNORANCE ONLY: BUSINESS IMMUNE SYSTEM REPORT	
	2: IGNORANCE
1: Management	C
2: Personnel	C
3: Production	B
4: Plant	B
5: Metrics	C
6: Marketing	F
7: Sales	F

WORKSHEET 8

IGNORANCE ONLY: BUSINESS IMMUNE SYSTEM REPORT	
	2: IGNORANCE
1: Management	
2: Personnel	
3: Production	
4: Plant	
5: Metrics	
6: Marketing	
7: Sales	

NOTES:

_____

_____

_____

EXAMPLE 9: INEPTITUDE ONLY: JOHNSON'S HARDWARE BISR

INEPTITUDE ONLY: BUSINESS IMMUNE SYSTEM REPORT	
	3: INEPTITUDE
1: Management	C
2: Personnel	C
3: Production	B
4: Plant	B
5: Metrics	C
6: Marketing	D
7: Sales	B

WORKSHEET 9

INEPTITUDE ONLY: BUSINESS IMMUNE SYSTEM REPORT	
	3: INEPTITUDE
1: Management	
2: Personnel	
3: Production	
4: Plant	
5: Metrics	
6: Marketing	
7: Sales	

NOTES:

_____

_____

_____

Notes

CHAPTER 1
1. W. Edwards Deming, Deming Four-Day Seminar, February 1993, Phoenix, AZ.
2. Atul Gawande, *The Checklist Manifesto: How to Get Things Right* (Gurgaon, India: Penguin Random House, 2014).

CHAPTER 3
1. Dave Ramsey, *EntreLeadership: 20 Years of Practical Business Wisdom from the Trenches* (New York: Howard Books, 2011).

CHAPTER 6
1. Henry Ford, Samuel Crowther, and William A. Levinson, *My Life and Work: Henry Ford's Universal Code for World-Class Success* (Boca Raton, FL: CRC Press, 2013).

CHAPTER 7
1. Harvey Mackay, *Swim with the Sharks Without Being Eaten Alive: Outsell, Outmanage, Outmotivate, and Outnegotiate Your Competition* (New York: HarperCollins, 2005).
2. Jim Collins, *Good to Great: Why Some Companies Make the Leap . . . and Others Don't* (New York: HarperCollins, 2001).

CHAPTER 9
1. Mike Michalowicz, *Profit First: Transform Your Business from a Cash-Eating Monster to a Money-Making Machine* (New York: Portfolio Penguin, 2017).

Index

About the Author

MATTHEW NEILL DAVIS OWNS AND MAN- ages Davis Law, PLLC, a firm dedicated to helping ambitious business owners become rock-star entrepreneurs. To do this, the firm finds solutions to pressing problems and runs custom legal departments for businesses and nonprofits. The firm proactively protects and improves businesses by removing legal hassles so that the owners and managers can focus on running their businesses. They do this by using the comprehensive, proprietary systems Davis developed while serving as general counsel for a range of companies. Currently the firm has offices in Oklahoma City; Tulsa; Wichita, Kansas; and Enid, Oklahoma, with plans for expansion. Davis Law has thrice made the Law Firm 500 for being among the fastest-growing law firms in the nation.

Davis lives in Enid, Oklahoma, where his family has lived for six generations, because he loves having ancestral farms and the three-minute commute. He is married to Allison Davis, a former producer for ABC in Los Angeles and an entrepreneur in her own right. They have five children, one adopted from Russia and one adopted from Ethiopia. They live in a very noisy, busy house. They have chalked up one National Merit Scholar to date. Davis holds a JD from the University of Oklahoma, an MPA from Cornell University, and a BSS from Cornell College.

Author photograph by Christina Mathews Photography